LOTHROP STODDARD
HARVARD CLASS OF 1905

This book collects the 2005 Lothrop Stoddard lectures, delivered by C. H. Dalton near Harvard University. The print edition is based on Dalton's original lecture notes, emending the text where necessary. Wherever possible, the editors have used Dalton's original slides as illustrations.

A
PRACTICAL
GUIDE
TO RACISM

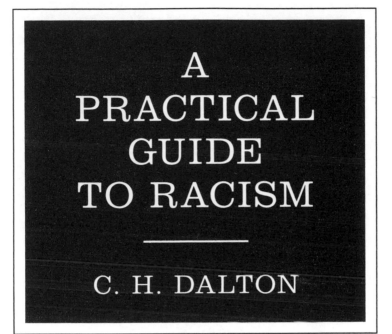

A PRACTICAL GUIDE TO RACISM

C. H. DALTON

ILLUSTRATIONS BY

Andy Friedman

Nicholas Gurewitch

Michael Kupperman

Sam Means

Tony Millionaire

R. Sikoryak

Liz Zanis

GOTHAM BOOKS

GOTHAM BOOKS

Published by Penguin Group (USA) Inc. 375 Hudson Street, New York, New York 10014, U.S.A.
Penguin Group (Canada), 90 Eglinton Avenue East, Suite 700, Toronto, Ontario M4P 2Y3, Canada
(a division of Pearson Penguin Canada Inc.); Penguin Books Ltd, 80 Strand, London WC2R 0RL,
England; Penguin Ireland, 25 St Stephen's Green, Dublin 2, Ireland (a division of Penguin Books
Ltd); Penguin Group (Australia), 250 Camberwell Road, Camberwell, Victoria 3124, Australia
(a division of Pearson Australia Group Pty Ltd); Penguin Books India Pvt Ltd, 11 Community Cen-
tre, Panchsheel Park, New Delhi–110–017, India; Penguin Group (NZ), 67 Apollo Drive, Rosedale,
North Shore 0632, New Zealand (a division of Pearson New Zealand Ltd); Penguin Books (South
Africa) (Pty) Ltd, 24 Sturdee Avenue, Rosebank, Johannesburg 2196, South Africa

Penguin Books Ltd, Registered Offices: 80 Strand, London WC2R 0RL, England

Published by Gotham Books, a member of Penguin Group (USA) Inc.

First printing, January 2008
1 3 5 7 9 10 8 6 4 2

Copyright © 2008 by Sam Means
Illustrations by Andy Friedman, Nicholas Gurewitch, Michael Kupperman,
Sam Means, Tony Millionaire, R. Sikoryak, Liz Yanis
All rights reserved

Gotham Books and the skyscraper logo are trademarks of Penguin Group (USA) Inc.

Library of Congress Cataloging-in-Publication Data
Dalton, C. H., 1954–
A practical guide to racism / C. H. Dalton; illustrations by Andy Friedman [et al.]
p. cm.
ISBN 978-1-592-40348-6 (hardcover)
1. Racism. 2. Race relations. I. Title.
HT1521.D35 2008
305.8—dc22
2007026037

Printed in the United States of America
Set in the modern style with the latest methods

FOR THE LADIES

CONTENTS

A
PRACTICAL
GUIDE
TO RACISM

INTRODUCTION

"The horse, the ass, the zebra, and the quagga are distinct species and distinct types: and so with the Jew, the Teuton, the Sclavonian, the Mongol, the Australian, the coast Negro, the Hottentot, &c."
—Josiah Clark Nott, *Types of Mankind*

The human race is not actually a race. It is a species, but it is divided into several convenient races, like Black, White, Asian, and Mixed. These divisions are based on subtle biological differences, and expressed physiologically in things like skin color, eye slantiness, and leg ashiness. *Racism* is the dislike of another race as a whole, or of another person solely because he is a member of a certain race.

As the title implies, this book is meant to serve as a practical guide to racism, for both racists and non-racists alike. It will explore the different stereotypes associated with members of different races and ethnic groups, as well as their origin and basis in fact. Are Swedish women really able to suck the chrome off a trailer hitch? No, of course not, but the stereotype is rooted in their extraordinary talent for oral sex.

We will also look at historical examples of racism, especially here in America, and the extent to which racism has been institutionalized or officially sanctioned,[1] but mostly we will be dealing with the use of stereotypes, epithets, and racial caricatures.

Like this one. This one doesn't even make sense.

Fig. 1. "An Irish Jig" Fig. 2. "The Irish Frankenstein"

The concept of race is controversial, since variation within the traditionally established races is often far more extreme than between any two ethnic groups, but to say that we don't divide each other into

1. "Representatives and direct Taxes shall be apportioned among the several States which may be included within this Union, according to their respective Numbers, which shall be determined by adding to the whole Number of free Persons, including those bound to Service for a Term of Years, and excluding Indians not taxed, three fifths of all other Persons." (Article 1, Section 2, Clause 3 of the United States Constitution)

races would be to ignore thousands of years of human history. Not to mention the fact that white people drive a car like *this*:

Fig. 3

While black people drive a car like *this*:

Fig. 4

Despite increasing globalization and intermarriage, or "miscegenation," there are still distinct and important differences between members of the different races. Since the subtlety and scope of those differences are far too complicated to be helpful to us in everyday life,

we employ certain heuristics, or "stereotypes," to better understand and more comfortably interact with those different from ourselves. Like the Maori.

Such stereotypes are sometimes controversial, because they can oversimplify the differences between individuals. Every person is different, and it is rare for someone to fit a stereotype perfectly. Except for so-called "walking stereotypes," like Carson from *Queer Eye*.[2] Others don't have *any* of the characteristics ascribed to their race in such stereotypes. It's an imperfect science at best.

For example, just because the Maori are, in general, lazy, selfish, and long-winded, that does not mean that noted Maori opera singer Kiri Te Kanawa is any of those things. In fact, she is only two of them, because she is a soprano, and sopranos tend to be very succinct.

Even so, stereotypes can be very useful in our everyday social interactions and decision-making. They are actually a kind of survival instinct—a crude form of received inductive reasoning that can help us make snap judgments in situations where we don't have all the facts.

When entering into a business deal with someone of *Roma* descent, for instance, I am very careful of my possessions. Knowing the stereotype that gypsies are tramps and thieves,[3] I am able to better protect myself when coming into contact with them, and my increased vigilance might save me from becoming a victim. At any moment, a baby could come flying at me and, when I catch it, a young, dark-haired girl will steal my camera.

(If you find yourself confronted with this particular scam, it is better to drop the baby. Another little known stereotype is that gypsy children are unusually sturdy.)

2. "Gay" is not, technically, one of the nine major races. Nonetheless, it receives due diligence in this book.

3. I'd hear it from the people of the town.

Similarly, if I were looking for someone to lend me money, a Jewish person would be unlikely to help me, because they are traditionally parsimonious. It is best not to even ask, at the risk of being subjected to one of their patented "guilt trips" or, worse, jewed out of what money I do have.[4]

That's why words like "jewed" and "gypped" exist. Are you calling Noah Webster a racist?

I bring this up because it is important to keep in mind the difference between stereotypes and racism. Stereotypes are a useful, if flawed, mechanism for surviving in a multicultural world, but racism is saying them out loud.

Racism is about more than just making impolitic comments, though; it is about hatred. Broad stereotypes often fuel racism, but merely believing a stereotype about another race doesn't make you a racist.[5] After all, some of my best friends are members of other races. So stereotypes are kind of a *sine qua non* of racism—a *without which not* of hating people different from yourself, if you will.

Racism doesn't need to stop at personal distaste, though. Many racists in positions of power have used their standing to oppress and even kill entire groups of people. I can't condone that kind of violence, but it's hard to argue with the science behind it. If eugenics and racialist phrenology have taught us nothing else, it's that we can, through selective breeding, eliminate all those with a pronounced ideality lump on their left temple.[6]

Being labeled a racist in today's society can be extremely damaging to your reputation and your career, whether you're a stand-up come-

4. If you are actually looking to borrow money, Laotians tend to be quite generous. However, you run the very real risk of getting raped.

5. For example, the SAT is not racist, even though it thinks that black people are less intelligent than white people. That's because the SAT is just a piece of paper, and not capable of having an emotion like hatred.

6. The Armenians.

dian, a movie star, or a radio host. And
if you're a true racist, minorities will
be able to tell. They have an innate
ability to sense when someone is being
racist, a kind of radar for racism that
I call "racism-dar," or "ra-dar."

This book is divided into nine chap-
ters, each devoted to a different ethnic
group: Jews, Asians, Whites, Blacks,
Gypsies, Indians (and Injuns), His-
panics, Arabs, and Merpeople,[7] and

Fig. 5

several appendices, including a glossary of racial epithets. Anyone
who's ever thought about dating outside his own race will surely
appreciate my guide to jungle fever, yellow fever, and the other vari-
ous and sundry fevers.

Within each chapter we will consider not just broad ethnic stereo-
types, like "South Africans are cowards," but more specific generalities
as well, like "Swazi men are meth-heads." Lazy Guatemalans and indus-
trious El Salvadorans are both covered in the chapter on Hispanics.

To sum up, racism is the hatred of members of another ethnic group
solely because of their race, and it is often informed by negative and
untrue stereotypes. It's okay to hate someone because of who they
are, but hating them because of their ethnicity alone is racist. Over the
next nine chapters we'll look at the history, etymology, and practical
applications of racism in this country today.

And just in case there was any confusion, the human race is not
actually a race, like a footrace, either. If it were, the blacks probably
would have won.

7. This is the modern division of the races, according to the latest scientific thought. The jury
 is still out on Cablinasians (see Appendix on "Questionable Races").

~~⌒~~

HISPANICS

A PRACTICAL GUIDE TO FECUNDITY

Now, more than ever, it is important to be familiar with our spicy neighbors to the south, the Hispanics.

Everyone's heard the stereotypes. "They like tacos." "They're tiny." "They have big ears and are often carried around in women's purses." But did you know that Hispanics, or "Mexicans," are also hardworking tradesmen and small businesspeople?[1] It's true.

Hispanics play an important role in American society, doing the work that Americans don't want to do, and secreting a pungent, waxy substance known as ambergris, which is used as a fixative in some expensive perfumes. An increased demand

Fig. 1. A typical Hispanic

1. For the purposes of this book, your lawn counts as a small business.

for cheap labor and high-end fragrances brings millions of Hispanics to the United States every year. And they squeeze out babies faster than the Latvians, so their numbers are only increasing. According to a recent study, by 2015 the population of the United States will be 78 percent Mexican.

U.S. POPULATION 2015

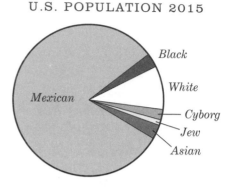

Fig. 2

That's why many are calling for immigration reform, to prevent more Hispanics from coming here and taking low-paying jobs away from real Americans. Though, in many cases, these are jobs that American workers are too lazy to do, like playing shortstop.

But who are these fence-hopping visitors from "down under," and do they deserve to be our scapegoats? Before we retroactively leap to judgment, it's important to learn more about the individuals who make up this new, Yellow-Brown Peril.

For starters, the Hispanics you see every day aren't your everyday Mexicans. Only the very highest achievers make it to America. After completing degree work in one of several fields, their final examination consists of an intensive obstacle course between their homes and the hinterlands of southern Texas. While these skilled, motivated Hispanics can find a wide variety of demeaning work here in America, in their home countries the vast majority of them must make a living by diving for oysters or pennies thrown into the water by tourists.

Of course, Hispanics can't work *all* the time. They also enjoy a variety of leisure pursuits, such as football, though they seem to be a lit-

tle unclear on the rules. They are also skilled baseball players, due to early, piñata-based training, and in the evening they amuse themselves by playing enormous, oversized guitars.[2] American music is popular, as well; just as Germans love David Hasselhoff and Iraqis can't get enough Lionel Richie, Hispanics are obsessed with the alt-pop stylings of songwriter Duncan Sheik.[3]

The stereotypes you tend to hear about Hispanics are, for the most part, accurate: they are a friendly people, prone to narcolepsy in the afternoon hours, and their women have phenomenal asses. Mexicans, sometimes called "Latin" or "Latino" for their love of Martial's epigrams, are also known throughout the world as wonderful lovers, but that is, unfortunately, not the case. **The Latin Lover** stereotype comes from the fact that Hispanic men are very successful seducers of women,[4] but when it comes to the actual mechanics of intercourse, they are woefully inadequate. This inability to satisfy their partners is the origin of the phrase *"dos pump chump."*

THE HISPANIC MIND

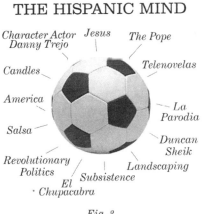

Character Actor Danny Trejo
Jesus
The Pope
Candles
Telenovelas
America
La Parodia
Salsa
Duncan Sheik
Revolutionary Politics
Landscaping
Subsistence
El Chupacabra

Fig. 3

Not all Hispanic people are alike, though, so before we go any further it's important to start looking at all the different kinds of Mexicans, like South Americans, Central Americans, Iberians, and Carabiners.

2. These guitars can also be used as makeshift boats in the event of a hasty emigration.

3. And, to a lesser extent, David Soul.

4. The odds are overwhelming that, at some time during your life together, a Hispanic person has plowed your wife.

THE HISPANIC WORLD

Have you ever wondered who that is down there mowing your lawn? What about the fellow over there cleaning your pool? And who's that young *chica* wiping fingerprints off the sliding door? Chances are they're all Hispanic, but that can mean a lot of different things.

Some things are common to all Mexicans. They all speak Spanglish, for example, and they all practice either voodoo or Catholicism.[5] But despite a common language, and love of switchblade knives, there are many regional subtleties that are not readily apparent to the lay non-Mexican.

By the way, if you don't know how to speak Spanglish, it's really quite easy: all you have to do is add "-o" to the end of every other word, and remember a few made-up ones like *"biblioteca"* and *"aquí."* It can even be fun to tell your contractor to "put the drywall-o *aquí,* not *aquí."* Be warned, though: It all seems relatively harmless now, but I'm told some extremist pro-Mexican *apologistas* actually want it taught in our schools. The last thing we need in academia is foreign languages other than Greek and Latin.

Hispanic countries are more than just a great place to assuage your white guilt by doing a year or two of ineffectual community service after college.[6] They are a rich collage of scary, foreign cultures. Let us now consider in turn the four regions of Hispania: Mexico, Central and South America, the Caribbean, and Iberia.

5. The differences between the two are not as stark as you might imagine.
6. I highly recommend doing this. It will give you something to talk about smugly for years to come.

MEXICO

Of the three countries in North America, this, the southernmost one, is where most Mexicans can be found. But, much like the killer bees never actually did, they are spreading into all areas of the United States.

Known for its energetic hat dancing, Mexico is actually a totalitarian oligarchy. It is governed by a group of Latin Kings, like Tarquin the Proud, who rule the country with an iron fist. They are not to be confused with the Latin Kings of Comedy, whose domain is limited to late-night filler on Comedy Central. Nor should they be confused with *Latin Inches*, which is a fine publication.

The Latin Kings' influence also extends to Mexican emigrants in America, which is troubling, because they seem to be extraordinarily tolerant of criminal behavior. Like much of the Hispanic world, Mexico is overrun with scofflaws and roustabouts, in addition to roving bands of lawless *banditos* (literally, "roving bands"). Of these, none was more fearsome than the ruthless Frito Bandito, who traveled the Mexican countryside in the early 1970s, robbing tourists of their salted corn chips.

But the most famous bandito was probably the revolutionary leader Pancho Villa. Villa was, of course, General John Pershing's white whale, which is ironic, because he was Mexican.

As with all races, it's important to be tolerant of Mexicans, but also vigilant, especially with your personal possessions. Unlike American law enforcement, the police in Mexico are overweight and corrupt. To give you an idea of just how bad it is, the Mexican *Law & Order* is only half an hour long, and usually ends in the beating death of an innocent suspect.

To be fair, their jobs are also more difficult than those of the American police. Mexicans, as a race, are very fleet-footed, or "speedy," and extremely diminutive in stature. They are almost rodent-like in

this respect. *"Arriba! Arriba!"* you can hear them cry, as they elude their pursuers.

Nonetheless, Mexican leaders and police seem ambivalent, especially about the overt criminal activities of the country's two most famous citizens, comedians Cheech Marin and Tommy Chong.[7] On one occasion, the pair even drove a van constructed entirely of marijuana from Mexico into the United States without being apprehended by law enforcement.

We will consider illegal narcotics in more detail below, but for a nuanced look at the role they play in Mexico, I recommend watching the movie *Traffic*. As with so many of the complicated issues that face the world today, the drug trade is best addressed by the subtle social commentary of director Steven Soderbergh.

GEOGRAPHY

Mexico is divided into thirty-one states, each ruled by a governor and legislature, much like in America, except that state politics in Mexico is overrun by cronyism and corruption. The border regions, like Baja California, are especially populous, and serve as a way station for immigrants passing into the United States. From Mexicali, for example, Mexicans cross over into the city of Calexico, California. This geographical situation is similar to the Helgium and Bolland areas in Western Europe.

The eastern states of Sonora and Chihuahua, on the other hand, send border-jumpers into Texas and the American Southwest, although many simply pass through on their way to the amber waves of grain

7. Marin is better known in this country for his role on the sitcom *The Golden Palace*.

in the Midwest, which they then hull for less than a quarter of mini- mum wage.

Further south, Mexico is known for its beach resorts, in towns like Cancún. They may appear to be idyllic coastal paradises, but travel- ers should be careful when visiting areas like Cancún and Cabo San Lucas. The girls there are untamed, and liable to go wild at a moment's notice. Often, they can be provoked by little more than the offer of a free hat, or a string of beads. Visitors to Cabo are likewise warned not to make eye contact with Sammy Hagar.

Fig. 4. Cabo Wabo

Mexico is also home to the feared Chupacabra, though its specific whereabouts are unknown. Much like film critic Roger Ebert, this mythical creature is active at night, when it stalks rural areas and sucks the blood of goats. The Chupacabra also cowrote the campy 1970 classic, Beyond the Valley of the Dolls with Russ Meyer.

THE LESSER AMERICAS

Don't let the name fool you; there is nothing American about the lower half of the Western Hemisphere. It is a lawless society, whose citizens are known to openly participate in a dance that is expressly forbidden by law.

Outside of the textile industry, there are no legitimate businesses operating in Southern or Central America at all.[8] Unlike in the United States, where it is a distant third, the number-one industry in the region is kidnapping. The kidnapping industry brings in a significant amount of foreign investment every year, mostly in non-sequential bills.

Of course, lawlessness is to be expected from a culture founded on crime, by a criminal. Simón Bolívar was the leader of the South and Central American independence movement, and is known as the "George Washington of South America," because he hated cherry trees. In the course of his revolutionary activities, he knowingly murdered hundreds of viceroys and colonial overlords in cold blood. It is not a stretch to see a direct line from a mountebank like Bolívar to the prevalence of gang violence among Hispanic youths.

Fig. 5. Business expense

Bolívar's mission is carried on today by other successful revolutionary leaders who also suck at running countries, like Daniel Ortega, Evo Morales, and Hugo Chávez. It's just a shame that the lower Americas are no longer ruled by people who know what's best for them, like the United Fruit Company.

Morales and Chávez are at the forefront of a brash new wave of Hispanic leaders not installed by the CIA. Chávez is a megalomaniac, but Morales seems to be an idealist, if an impractical one, and he's done wonderful things for alpaca.

The lower Americas are known for more than just their politics,

8. Textiles are a large part of the economy in many areas, like the Patagonia region of South America, which is known for its synthetic fleece.

Fig. 6. El Presidente Cosby

though. They have also been home to great writers, like Colombia's Gabriel García Márquez, Peru's Mario Vargas Llosa,[9] and Argentina's Jorge Luis Borges, the world's most famous ADHD sufferer. And who can forget the great Argentinean actor, Manu Ginóbili? Over the years, his exaggerated pratfalls have delighted millions.

ORIGINAL WORKING TITLES FOR
GABRIEL GARCÍA MÁRQUEZ'S
LOVE IN THE TIME OF CHOLERA

Love in the Time of Gout
Love in the Time of Herpes Simplex I
Love in the Time of Eczema
Love in the Time of Ovarian Cancer
Love in the Time of Old People Having Sex

Brazil, meanwhile, is home to the most beautiful women in the entire world. Which may explain why there aren't many men from Brazil who have accomplished anything.

THE CARIBBEAN

While they are not as hardworking as many other Hispanics, since they spend most of their time helping white tourists procure marijuana, Carabiners are accomplished cooks and shipbuilders.

9. Not to be confused with Alberto Vargas, the Peruvian artist revered by hipster masturbators everywhere.

In addition to figuring out ways to make goat palatable, Caribbean cooks have discovered a secret recipe that makes anything delicious. All you need to do is slather it in jerk sauce. It works for meat, fish, vegetables, fruits, and even other condiments. This author could happily eat a dinner of jerk apples with a side of jerk mayonnaise any day of the week.[10]

When they are not cooking exotic, spicy dishes, there is nothing Carabiners love more than boating. They make ships out of everything from driftwood, to bathtubs, to 1950s-era pickup trucks, so that they can go on leisurely pleasure cruises under cover of night.

Hispanics in Cuba might want to spend more time on dry land, if they were not ruled by a tyrant like Fidel Castro. He will probably be dead by the time you read this, but it will not be soon enough. Unfortunately, the great Batista died in exile in 1973, so there will be no return to the glory days Cuba enjoyed under his rule.

Instead, many Cubans attempt to escape to America, where they turn to crime. It's a well-established career path: First, they earn the money. Then they use that money to achieve the power until, finally, they are able to get the women. Eventually, these Cuban émigrés control their own criminal empires, then become hubristic and paranoid, and are finally toppled by their own cocaine-inflated sense of self-worth. It's the classic American immigrant's tale.

Cuba, like most of the islands in the Caribbean, is an independent nation, free to be oppressed in whatever way they choose, but there are still a few British, Dutch, and French holdings, and Puerto Rico is owned by the United States. It does not have statehood, though, or a vote in Congress, so it is still merely a colonial possession, like the District of Columbia.

10. Unfortunately, my personal chef is French, so I am forced to make do with cold potato soup.

It does, however, have a parade every year in New York City, when Puerto Rican immigrants take to the streets to dance, eat, and scare the living crap out of Upper East Side Jews.

IBERIA

Just as Africa is the motherland of the African Americans, all Hispanics can trace their ancestry back to the Iberian Peninsula. And in 1968, Iberia got the ultimate stamp of legitimacy: a book by James Michener.

The bulk of Iberia, both geographically and culturally, is Spain, which is best known for its delicious signature foods: omelets, rice, and peanuts. And the Spanish, like their peanuts, are oily, tan, and cause allergic reactions in 1 to 2 percent of children.

Spain is also famous for its art and music, especially its unique, Spanish style of playing the classical guitar. The greatest of the guitar virtuosos was the Spanish nobleman, Andrés Segovia. That's why he's known as "the Iberian Steve Vai." The artist Pablo Picasso is also from Spain, and many people believe that his juvenile scrawling was quite good.

Proletarian Spaniards are not as culturally inclined, however, and most of them exhibit pugilistic, rather than artistic, talents. But instead of the but-

Fig. 7. Joins Alaska, Caribbean, Chesapeake, Hawaii, Mexico, Poland, Space, Tales of the South Pacific, Texas, *and* James Michener's Own Puckered Asshole

Fig. 8. The great Spanish guitarist Henry Kissinger

terfly knives and shivs of their countrymen in the new world, Spaniards prefer a curved sword known as an *estoque*. It's a pastime that can turn deadly when they come face-to-face with their natural enemy, the male cow.

The Spanish are also accident-prone, which is why the entire city of Barcelona is childproofed. The right-angle-averse Catalonians all live in lumpy, curved buildings, so they are never in danger of running into a sharp corner, or a building that doesn't look like it's made out of sculpted mud.

The Portuguese are more difficult to classify. Unlike most Hispanics, they are actually small colonies of polyps that have the appearance of a single organism. Many people mistake them for jellyfish, but they are more properly classified as *siphonophora*, which is very different. It's impor-

Fig. 9. Gaudy

tant to be very careful when handling the Portuguese, since their tentacles contain an extremely poisonous toxin that can be released on contact. They are truly men of war.

An ocean may separate them from the rest of the Hispanic world, but the nations of Iberia are still actively involved in its affairs. In the Americas, every corner bodega sells international phone cards so that Hispanics can keep in touch with their ancestors back home in Spain, Portugal, and Andorra. The Iberian Peninsula also plays a vital role in an intercontinental triangle trade with South America and the United States.

While Iberia is technically involved in the Hispanic drug trade through this arrangement, the illegal activity occurs only in the Americas. That's why, instead of tackling the social issues involved, or allevi-

Fig. 10

ating the extreme poverty that leads people to use and sell drugs, the United States government has cannily decided to declare all-out war on a semi-arbitrary class of substances.

THE WAR ON DRUGS

President Richard Nixon declared war against illegal narcotics, and that war was further escalated by Ronald Reagan in the 1980s.[11] Illegal drugs are defined, of course, as anything that makes you feel good except alcohol and tobacco.[12] While less successful than the Kennedy

11. Just because it's morning in America doesn't mean you can wake and bake.
12. And, of course, any of the safe, legal drugs manufactured by our country's pharmaceutical industry.

administration's War on Monogamy, the War on Drugs has outlasted it by more than two decades.

It used to be that drug addicts were treated in hospitals, or with counseling, but conservatives have hit on a much more successful treatment: extensive prison sentences. If it weren't for mandatory minimums, these criminals would be back on the street in no time, taking drugs and setting a bad example for young people, and the numbers don't lie. There are more people in prison for possession now than ever before, so therefore we must be winning.

The War on Drugs also extends into the Hispanic world itself, where the majority of America's cocaine, heroin, and marijuana originates. The drugs are farmed and refined in Mexico and the lower Americas, and those that aren't are often smuggled through them. To bring the drugs to America, the smugglers frequently use a mule—the sterile offspring of a male donkey and a female horse—but some drug traffickers actually get people to swallow condoms full of drugs.

Once the drugs enter the country, American Hispanics take over and sell them to cool kids, musicians, and Hollywood actors. Most drugs come into the United States this way, except for crack cocaine, which is cooked in an enormous microwave deep beneath the CIA. This drug epidemic is just one more reason that we need to take a hard look at America's immigration problem.

THE IMMIGRATION DEBATE

If pedophiles were streaming across the border and settling in our country, Congress would have taken action a long time ago,[13] but they

13. And they did, when they stopped giving new visas to Tongans. Sick, island-dwelling fucks.

seem unwilling to do anything about the Mexicans. Every day, thousands of them enter this country illegally, crossing the border from Mexico, the Caribbean, Iberia, and across the Bering Strait. They bring their criminal tendencies and lascivious dance music to America, and there doesn't seem to be anything our government can do.

For years, security on the border between the United States and Mexico was lax, because, until recently, all scientific evidence suggested that Mexicans couldn't swim. Therefore, it was assumed that the Rio Grande was more than enough of a defense against illegal immigration. However, it turns out that Mexicans are excellent swimmers, so we've had to step up our efforts.[14]

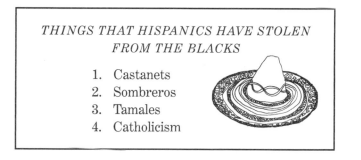

THINGS THAT HISPANICS HAVE STOLEN FROM THE BLACKS

1. Castanets
2. Sombreros
3. Tamales
4. Catholicism

Leading the charge have been the Minutemen, a group of Revolutionary War heroes come back from the dead to protect our borders once again. Just as they kept the invading Britons out of New England in the eighteenth century, they are now doing their best to keep out the invading Mexicans. Except instead of oppressive colonial rulers, the enemies this time are desperately poor manual laborers seeking a better life for themselves and their families. The bottom line is, the

14. Apparently we were thinking of chimps.

Minutemen are doing important work protecting America from all the things they originally fought to protect back in 1776.

Some people have proposed building a giant wall to keep the Hispanics out, and placing Lou Dobbs in the guard tower with a high-powered sniper rifle. This might work, but we also need more men patrolling the border, and that's just the beginning. In my weekly letter to the Depart-

Fig. 11. Back from the dead to protect our borders once again.

ment of the Interior, I have suggested a number of different solutions to the problem of illegal immigration from the south. Here are just a few ideas:

- Land mines
- Wall of flame
- Invisible fence (this plan would also require us to outfit all Mexicans with electronic collars)
- Tectonic shift to separate the United States from Mexico
- Chemical castration
- Making all Hispanics wear small brown stars, in order to more easily tell them apart

All reasonable plans of action, but there are some crackpots out there, too. These crazies believe that, instead of closing our borders,

we should throw our time and money down the toilet on "progressive" solutions. What exactly do we have to gain by improving Mexico's infrastructure, or alleviating the social injustice that leads people to come here illegally in the first place? The Hispanic world needs to take care of itself, and when Mexico stands up, we will take our giant wall down.

The outcry over Hispanic workers taking away jobs glosses over the real problem here. I am speaking, of course, of the lazy American poor. If working-class Americans would just work harder for less money, this wouldn't even be an issue. That is the lesson of globalization.[15]

CONCLUSION

It's not the Hispanics' fault that they are willing to work harder for less than all the lazy, entitled American people living below the poverty line, but that doesn't mean that we want them in this country. While there are some exceptional, talented Hispanics (e.g., Julio Iglesias, Enrique Iglesias, Julio Iglesias, Jr.), most of them are uneducated and criminally inclined. To add insult to injury, Hispanic lawbreakers are also more diligent and industrious than American criminals.

15. Of course, this isn't an issue for non-menial laborers. I'd like to see a Mexican take over a job teaching at a world-class research university.

FURTHER READING

If you're interested in learning more about the Hispanic peoples, here are some suggestions for further reading:

Mencia, Carlos. *Beaner!* HarperCollins, 2005.

Lopez, George, and Paul Rodriguez. *Beaners!* Random House, 2003.

Green, Aliza. *Beans: 200 Delicious, Wholesome Recipes.* Running Press, 2004.

JEWS

*A PRACTICAL GUIDE TO EVERYTHING WRONG
IN YOUR LIFE AND WHY IT'S THEIR FAULT*

You would be hard-pressed to find a group as hated or oppressed throughout history as the Jews. As John Lennon said, "Jews are the nigger of the world."

But has that hatred been justified? Yes and no.

The Hebrews are an intelligent, hardworking people, but in many countries they are ostracized for taking jobs away from non-immigrants. And whatever goodwill remains is often squandered when they are caught drinking the blood of Christian babies. As a people, their industriousness is matched only by their thirst for the blood of Christian babies. For better or worse, that is the history of the Jewish people.

Many Jews object to the very idea of a Jewish ethnic identity. They

claim that Judaism is a faith, not a race. But then these same people believe that Jewishness is passed down matrilineally. What the fuck kind of sense does that make?

The answer is "none."

That doesn't mean that all Jewish people look alike, of course. Not all Jews have curly hair and big noses, like Howard Dean's wife, Judith, but as

Fig. 1. Howard Dean and his wife, Judith Steinberg Dean

Supreme Court Justice Potter Stewart said of hard-core pornography, "I know it when I see it."[1]

You can convert to Judaism, but you have to be born Jewish, and that is the essence of race. For the most part, at least—it is possible to become black later in life, but it is offensive to do so.[2]

With all the hearsay and rumor surrounding a race like the Jews, there are bound to be misconceptions. During the Middle Ages, they were even accused of causing the bubonic plague by poisoning wells in European towns, but that is simply not true. The plague was started by a bunch of filthy rats: the Portuguese. Anyway, if the Jews had wanted to spread a plague, they would have used witchcraft.

That's not to say that they are blameless. According to noted

1. *Buttfuck Sluts Go Nuts v. Ohio* (1964).

2.

scholar Professor Griff, "Jews are responsible for the majority of wickedness that goes on across the globe."[3] But it's still important to separate fact from fiction.

For example, they may have big noses, curly hair, and prehensile tails, but whatever you may have heard, *Jews do not have horns.* I don't even know how this hurtful stereotype ever got started. The Jew's horns are *vestigial* and, in most modern cases, barely noticeable.

Fig. 2. The esteemed professor

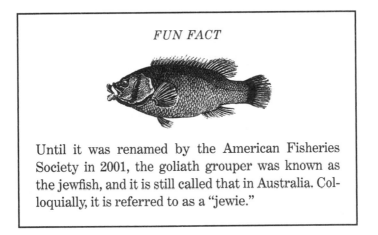

FUN FACT

Until it was renamed by the American Fisheries Society in 2001, the goliath grouper was known as the jewfish, and it is still called that in Australia. Colloquially, it is referred to as a "jewie."

HISTORY

Slanderous lies like these have contributed to millennia of hatred and violence against the Jews. The Jews are called the "chosen people" because they were chosen by God for thousands of years of persecu-

3. Professor Richard "Professor Griff" Griffin is an expert in the Semitic race. He is, perhaps, most famous for his insight, "Is it a coincidence that the Jews run the jewelry business and it's called 'jewelry'? No coincidence."

tion, and that discrimination continues to this day. According to the Anti-Defamation League, more than 100 percent of all words spoken in the world today are anti-Semitic.

They've been so persecuted that they've had to resort to inventing fictional characters to save them, like the Prague Golem and their so-called "Messiah." Is it any surprise that two Jews created Superman? A race as physically frail and prone to enuresis as the Jews hasn't had much luck standing up for itself.

It is that unique combination of sissiness and worldly success that has made them the target of innumerable pogroms, genocides, and blood libels.

"Blood libel" is really a misnomer, though, since Webster's defines libel as a statement or representation "that conveys an unjustly unfavorable impression." And while the accusation that Jews drink the blood of Christian babies certainly conveys an unfavorable impression, it is hardly unjust.

It is no more libelous than a statement like "Anthony Quinn was a pedophile," or "Naomi Wolf did porn."[4] Unfavorable, sure, but 100 percent true.

Fig. 3. The Jewish feast of "Passover"

According to longtime Catholic doctrine, attested to by Saint Simon, it is Jewish ritual practice to kidnap and torture a Christian child, then sentence him to death in a mock tribunal. The child is then crowned with thorns and

4. There's no denying that she has the aura of election upon her.

nailed to a wooden cross (a popular way for Jews to kill people), and his blood collected in bowls in order to drink it. As a goodwill gesture, the Pope repudiated this story in 1965, which was a very, very long time ago. Now only Arabs and a few brave racists believe the truth.

But enough about how much Jews like drinking the blood of Christian babies (a lot). Even before the Middle Ages, Jews faced widespread institutional prejudice. The Jews were once slaves of the ancient Egyptians, and helped to build their pyramids.

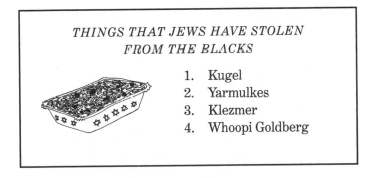

> **THINGS THAT JEWS HAVE STOLEN FROM THE BLACKS**
>
> 1. Kugel
> 2. Yarmulkes
> 3. Klezmer
> 4. Whoopi Goldberg

According to historian Erich von Däniken, the Jews teamed up with super-intelligent space aliens who provided them with the technology and know-how to build the Egyptian pyramids.[5] Mere humans could never have been able to complete such massive, architecturally advanced structures on their own.

More recently, Jews have been subject to wholesale expulsion from England and France, torture and inquisition in Spain, and laws in Germany prohibiting intermarriage with Christians for people with at least one Jewish grandparent (Octa-Jews are still okay). But frankly,

5. Von Däniken has proved conclusively that the gods were astronauts.

the Jews didn't want to live in their crappy countries, anyway, or marry their crappy daughters, or not be tortured.

Then, in the middle of the twentieth century, a frustrated painter named Adolf Hitler allegedly killed six million European Jews. Which, if true, would have been the worst thing ever done by an artist until Robert Longo directed *Johnny Mnemonic*.[6]

So, six million fewer for whatever reason, wearing their snappy yellow stars and *judenhuts*,[7] in May 1948 the Jews formed their own country: Israel.

Now that they've got their own country, things are much more peaceful. The Jews haven't been the targets of genocide for more than sixty years now, and it's rare that suicide bombers blow up more than

Fig. 4. A group, or "cabal," of Jews wearing their cool new hats

Fig. 5. Another (photo © Allan Tannenbaum)

6. Rimshot.

7. Special hats Jews were forced to wear, literally meaning "Jew hat." Seriously.

two or three buses full of them in any given month. But that sterling record doesn't mean that hurtful stereotypes don't still exist today.

SOME COMMON JEWISH STEREOTYPES

Historically, one of the most frequently cited stereotypes among anti-Semites is that of the **Covetous Jew,** who is obsessed with money and will do anything to get it. The covetous Jew is often a usurer or a dealer in diamonds or precious metals. Despite his strong ties to family and community, and a rich cultural heritage, he is a slithering, heartless snake who will cheat you out of your last dollar and rape your wife with his forked penis in order to collect the outrageous interest on his dirty loans. He is also a skilled tailor.

Fig. 6. The covetous Jew, captured here in mid-scheme.

How do stereotypes like this one get started? In the case of the covetous Jew, it all goes back to the Hebrew's unquenchable thirst for money and gold. Of course, Jews these days are only covetous for power. And, in the younger generations, Asian women.

More common today is the **Self-Hating Jew**. Jews have been oppressed and abused for so long that some of them have internalized that persecution. Perhaps the most extreme manifestation of this occurred 2,000 years ago, when they famously killed one of their own, the so-called "King of the Jews." But the internalization of years of oppression and their racial guilt over killing the son of God are just

two of the many, many reasons Jews have to hate themselves. That's why so many of them are cutters.

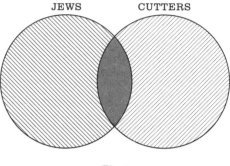

Fig. 7

They have to cut themselves just to feel.

One specific incarnation of the self-hating Jew is the **Nebbish**.[8] The nebbish's self-hatred manifests itself in neurotically fumbling with his glasses and making pretentious literary references, then realizing that he's being pretentious and trying to talk his way out of it, but only coming off worse in the process. His movies tend to be ploddingly self-referential, but he will be able to coast forever on the strength of his early brilliance.

Such neuroses aren't purely culturally received, though. Very often they come from being raised by a **Jewish Mother**. The stereotypical Jewish mother is overprotective, passive-aggressive, and a little hippy. She rules her home with an iron fist and utterly, utterly emasculates her husband and all male children.

It was not always so, though. Every Jewish mother was once a **Jewish American Princess (JAP)**. The JAP is a spoiled, nasal, and

8. Most nebbishes live here in America, rather than Israel, and the vast majority of them are in New York City. That's why Jesse Jackson called it "Hymietown."

kind-of-slutty young Jewish girl, who can pass for either Italian or Puerto Rican with the right accessories. Once beloved as actual princesses, JAPs have been universally reviled ever since December 7, 1941, when they bombed Pearl Harbor.

Fig. 8. One of the tools of the Jewish mother

It was a day that will live in infamy, and a *shonda* for the *goyim*.

While they rarely interact with outsiders, you've probably seen an **Orthodox Jew** altering clothes, sitting in a steam room, or offering you a bargain on something or other. These bearded, Jewish ninjas are known for their black clothes, extreme stealth, and *peyot*.[9] Orthodox women, on the other hand, wear wigs.

One of the most insidious anti-Semitic stereotypes is the myth of the **Red-Haired Jew**. The very notion of a Jew having red, curly hair is offensive to both Jews and people with red hair. This entirely false stereotype goes back to the eighteenth century, when the English would construct homemade effigies of Jews on the third Saturday of every April, the feast day of St. Killjews.

The only color of paint available to many poorer Britons was a bright crimson red, which they used to draw the effigies' features, like big noses and curly hair. They would then beat these straw-stuffed Hebrews with sticks and set them on fire.

In the days surrounding the holiday, it wasn't uncommon to hear the parents of uncooperative British children threaten to punish them in the same manner as those effigies. "If you don't clean your room, Nigel," they'd say, "I'll beat you like a red-headed Jew!" The colloquialism was so common that it spread across Europe, and created the

9. Curly fries.

myth of a hideous, red-haired Jew who never has and never will exist.

Not all stereotypes about Jews are false, though, or even negative. For example, everyone knows that Jews control the media. But did you know that, while Fox News and Aljazeera are controlled by a small group of self-hating Jews, the rest of the media is owned and run by a single Semite? Maxicronicus is the last survivor of an ancient race of vampires, and he also happens to be Jewish.

Not all Jews are vampires, of course. In fact, Maxicronicus is the only known Jewish vampire, and he only converted for his first wife, Rachel. Most Jews don't drink blood at all, except on religious holidays, so if you're not a Christian baby you don't have anything to worry about.

A similar stereotype that is, likewise, only partly true is that Jews are zombies. This is based on a common logical fallacy: Yes, all zombies are Jews (Christians go to heaven or hell, while Jews are doomed to roam the earth for eternity), but that does not mean that all Jews are zombies.

Fig. 9. The classic stereotype of the cowboy Jew

Fig. 10. Maxicronicus's true form is unknown, but scholars believe he may have inhabited the bodies of prominent humans since the dawn of man.

This chart should help you tell the difference between Jews and zombies.

	JEWS	ZOMBIES
What they want	Money	Brains
Skin color	Olive	Green
Method of transference	Matrilineal	Bites
How to kill them	Gunshot to the head	Gunshot to the head
Greatest fear	Pogroms	Fire
Natural enemies	Nazis	The living
Lifespan	77 years	Indefinite
Place of worship	Synagogue	Brains

If you're still confused, just remember that zombies tend to walk around saying "braaains" in a bloodless monotone, while most Jews don't.[10]

CONCLUSION

Historically, the Jews have been the most consistently and ardently hated race in the world. And it's because they killed Jesus.

10. Except the Lubavitch.

FURTHER READING

If you're interested in learning more about the Jewish people, here is a suggestion for further reading:

Anonymous. *The Protocols of the Learned Elders of Zion.* Victor Marsden, trans. Liberty Bell Publications, 1976.

CHAPTER THREE

<!-- decorative divider -->

WHITES

A PRACTICAL GUIDE TO RACISTS

"White" is a very broad term. It encompasses people from many different countries and backgrounds, from Americans to southerners to the Irish. Also, Polacks.

To many, it seems like a misnomer. After all, aren't most white people more of a pinkish hue? In some racial theory, white is not a race at all, but rather the absence of race. It follows that all colored peoples are ethnic others, and whites are a base or norm around which the races revolve. Not surprisingly, this is the view held by most whites, and, until 1962, by the Crayola company.

However, elementary color theory teaches us that white is not the absence of color, but the presence of *all* colors, and that's why white people are so insecure. Just imagine all the bad things about Jews,

blacks, Asians, Injuns, and the gays wrapped up in one pasty, freckled package.[1]

Whites hate all other races, but it is only because, in truth, they hate themselves; it is the white man's racial self-loathing that feeds his inveterate racism. We always hate most about other people what we most despise in ourselves. So the white man ("The Man") may enslave entire peoples and colonize their homelands, but he does so with his face hidden under a white hood, and at night he cries himself to sleep.

But just as with feuding siblings, there is still love between the races. Plantation owners and third presidents frequently impregnated black women in the south, and no one did it classier than South Carolina Dixiecrat Strom Thurmond.

STROM THURMOND: AMERICAN PATRIOT

Fig. 1. Down with the swirl

Not long before he ran for president on a segregationist platform, Strom was regularly boning his family's colored maid in the upstairs broom closet. At the time, the young racist was suffering from a medical condition known as "jungle fever," which cleared up as soon as he was elected to public office in South Carolina.

Strom's congress with sixteen-year-old Carrie Butler produced a daughter, Essie Mae Washington-Williams, whom he kept

1. No, *thank you.*

a secret for almost eighty years.[2] While providing financial support to his illegitimate black daughter, the then-senator performed the longest filibuster in Senate history in an attempt to derail the Civil Rights Act of 1957. Now that's tough love.

When he died in 2003, at the age of one hundred, Thurmond was the oldest living Confederate maid-fucker.

While it's true that most whites are hypocrites and statutory rapists, not every white person is a bad guy. Notable Caucasians like John F. Kennedy, Robert Kennedy, and John F. Kennedy, Jr., were each, in their own way, "one of the good ones," and most white women are nice enough. Even your average cracker

Fig. 2. Fraternity hazing at Bob Jones University

isn't about to go out and lynch someone just for being different. That's because white supremacy is tempered in most white people by overwhelming *white guilt*. Guilt and racism are the *yin* and *yang* of the white mind.

At this point I feel I should mention that I am, myself, Caucasian. Which should come as no surprise, since I am a tenured professor at

2. That means that Strom Thurmond had a *real* illegitimate black child in South Carolina three-quarters of a century before John McCain had a made-up one.

a top-tier university. I only bring this up in the interest of full disclosure, because, for the purposes of my research, I am a scholar first and foremost, and a white person third.[3] I am writing this book in order to debunk the racist myths that pervade our society, not to perpetuate them, except when they are true.

HISTORY

The white race has a proud history of achievement and violence going back to the very dawn of civilization. White people in ancient Greece invented democracy and pederasty,[4] while whites in Germany later figured out a way to make soap out of people.

Just as the Jews gave the world "Sweet Caroline" and "Cracklin' Rosie," the whites have made significant contributions to our shared cultural history, in music (Elvis Presley's "In the Ghetto"), drama (Oscar Hammerstein's *Showboat*), movies (Michael Bay's *Bad Boys* and Michael Bay's *Bad Boys II*), and puppetry (Burr Tillstrom's *Kukla, Fran, and Sambo*). The main difference is, unlike the Jews, whites actually *do* control the world.

*THINGS WHITES HAVE STOLEN
FROM THE BLACKS*

1. Rock and roll
2. Fried chicken
3. Tap dancing
4. Their dignity

3. I am a Freemason second.
4. The Romans only held on to one of those two things.

And what would the world look like today if white people hadn't been around to make bland, soulless versions of the cuisine and culture of the other races? Probably a lot like one of those dangerous, ungentrified neighborhoods you wouldn't want to find yourself in after dark.

Perhaps the white's greatest talent is his ability as a mimic. Like the mynah bird and the copycat fox, whites can mimic any other race with perfect verisimilitude. With only a little face paint and a representative costume, whites like Al Jolson, C. Thomas Howell, and Robert Van Winkle have flawlessly portrayed members of other ethnicities on stage and screen. I dare you to tell the difference between Vanilla Ice and an actual black person.

Whites are also first-rate hockey players, investment bankers, and brewer-patriots, but they are hampered in other pursuits by a crippling inability to jump. They are simply unable to do it. That is why there will never be a truly great white triple jumper.[5]

But this shortcoming has pushed the white man to test the bounds of technology, creating motorized jumping machines like space shuttles, jetpacks, and moon shoes to make up for his physical shortcomings. These rocketeers and hover-skateboarders are proof of the white man's insuperable derring-do.

Perhaps the greatest example of the white man's indomitable spirit is Robert

Fig. 3. Regent University is known for its championship basketball team, the White Devils.

5. World record–holder Jonathan Edwards is actually a triple-jumping robot cleverly designed to look like a white person.

"Evel" Knievel. Knievel was born in Butte, Montana, in 1938, and over-came a lifetime of petty crime and insurance salesmanship to jump over stuff while riding a motorcycle—truly, man's highest purpose.

And, despite their racial handicap, many whites have nonetheless excelled at non-motorsports, as well. You can't open a newspaper these days without reading about white superstar athletes like Derek Jeter, Jason Kidd, and journeyman quarterback Charlie Batch.

Fig. 4. The evolution from non-whites to whites

Whites are originally from northern Europe, but their adventur-ous spirit led to them to explore beyond its borders at a very early stage. Also, being white, it was important for them to spread their objectively correct moral and religious schemata to the savage entire-rest-of-the-world. It was in those backward enclaves that they encoun-tered non-whites for the first time, and, armed only with superior weapons and armor, the whites heroically conquered the rest of the world and its many ethnic others. The European nations equitably split all the other countries and their peoples among themselves, and everything has been pretty much perfect since then.

However, after approximately 4,000 years in charge, the white man

has now been marginalized. Whites are under siege from a program known as affirmative action. Since the 1960s affirmative action has decimated the white population, and continues to whittle away at this once-proud race.

The program works by giving jobs and college educations to non-whites, even though they'll probably just use them to buy drugs. Experts believe that, if affirmative action continues at its current pace, purebred whites will be extinct by the year 2035, leaving only minorities and cockroaches.

DISCRIMINATION

Affirmative action is just one example of something called "reverse racism," so named because whites are the only ones who are allowed to be racist. Kind of like how the movie *Disclosure* was about reverse sexual harassment.

One of the ugliest examples of reverse racism is the minstrel show, in which black performers, most often Wayanses, chalk their faces with a substance known as face-white and gambol across the stage in a gross caricature of white behavior. They neurotically check their BlackBerries and listen to smooth jazz, while tucking their T-shirts into their pants and dancing arrhythmically. It is entertainment—and cruelty—of the lowest sort.

Of course, whites are no strangers to persecution. As John Lennon said, "Whites are the nigger of the world."

Whites may believe that they are superior to other races, but that's the sort of egotism that only comes from insecurity. And that inse-

curity has been bred by millennia of anti-white discrimination. Conquered peoples can be so cruel.

The earliest known example of reverse racism occurred in caveman times, when whites were persecuted by the dinosaurs. The early whites, clad only in saber-toothed tiger pelts, lived in constant fear of being lynched

Fig. 5. Artist's rendering

and eaten by one of these prehistoric bigots.

After the brontosaurus and his hateful ilk[6] received their comeuppance from God in the form of a giant asteroid, new races emerged to take their place: equally hateful, though warmer-blooded and slightly less imposing.

When white explorers discovered the Americas, the people who were living there at the time viciously persecuted the Europeans by refusing to give up their land. Apparently, Big Chief Selfish-pants had never heard of Manifest Destiny.

Whites in darkest Africa faced similar hurdles. As a minority, they were frequently discriminated against by cannibals, who would boil them in large pots, safari hats and all. However, due to the fact that the whites had guns, no civil rights movement was necessary.[7]

6. All those dinosaurs look the same to me.
7. Other races could learn a lesson from this.

A civil rights movement *was* necessary in the American South, where whites were segregated from other races—often forcibly—until as recently as the 1960s. They had to go to different schools, drink from different water fountains, and even sit in different parts of the same bus. They were separate, but rarely equal.

It all started in 1896, when the United States Supreme Court ruled to allow segregation in railway cars. *Plessy v. Ferguson* effectively

Fig. 6. The Coltrane Court

sanctioned institutional reverse racism, and was decided unanimously by the short-lived, all-minority Coltrane Court of the late nineteenth century. Nonetheless, the ruling stood until the 1950s.

Of course, *Brown v. Board* wasn't the end of anti-white discrimination in this country, as we've seen. Affirmative action continues to keep

the white man down, and a long tradition of raunchy black comedians, from Eddie Murphy to Eddie Griffin, has made a living with its vicious, anti-white humor. Well, there's nothing funny about that kind of bigotry, as anyone who has watched *Undercover Brother* can attest.

MEET THE OTHER WHITES

It may surprise you to hear that not all whites are intellectuals from the Northeast. It certainly came as a shock to me when I encountered my first hillbilly, but it's true; many white people were not even educated in the Ivy League. Whites can also be drunken Irishmen, drunken Russians, and even drunken Okies.

Before we look at the different kinds of whites, it's important to dispel some myths about the white man. For starters, the Holocaust never happened. Germans have been taking flack about this for years now, but there's no real evidence to support it. For all we know, those Jews just picked up and moved, and left their bones in mass graves in the German and Polish countryside.

Fig. 7. A 1929 charcoal drawing by the frustrated artist

The idiom "worse than Hitler" just refers to the young Austrian's lack of skill as a painter. Seriously, he was terrible. That's probably why all the anger and the yelling. Guy couldn't paint a happy little tree to save his life.

Also, contrary to popular belief, there *has* been a white president

of the United States. In fact, there have been forty of them. The only non-white presidents were John F. Kennedy (Catholic), Bill Clinton (black), and Millard Fillmore (Samoan).[8] All three shamed the office with their frequent and lascivious congress with white women, and that is why there will never be another.

And finally: Yes, Jesus was white as snow.

SOUTHERNERS, MIDWESTERNERS, CALIFORNIANS, AND POOR PEOPLE

Those American whites *not* from the wealthy enclaves of the Northeast are a strange breed. Most live in shotgun shacks[9] and work on dirt farms, when they have jobs at all. After they come home and boil the dirt they've farmed, they spend the rest of the evening fornicating with any and all available relatives and pets.

To take a break from all that incest and bestiality, and incestuous bestiality, they turn on the TV and watch a wealthy, private school–educated comedian named Dan Whitney, who pretends to be a cable repairman, and yet is somehow also a health inspector. I don't entirely understand it, myself.

Sometimes these non-wealthy non-Northeasterners ("white trash") manage to stumble out of their shantytowns and trailer parks and Napa Valleys in order to vote, but most of the time they occupy themselves with basic cable, pornography, and the occasional trip to the demolition derby or ultimate fighting match. It's best to avoid white

8. James Garfield was technically a mountain wolf, but he was a *white* mountain wolf.
9. Small houses composed of two barrels, one of which serves as the bedroom and the other as the bathroom.

trash if at all possible, but if you need to buy gas or rent a donkey from one, it's still a good idea to keep your distance. The smell of body odor and boiled peanuts can be overwhelming.

And the rest of the world is even worse.

BRITISH ISLANDERS

England, Scotland, and Ireland are filled to the brim with white people, and not the good kind, either. Though the English themselves are actually fairly palatable, and can make a mean *tikka masala*. They are a refined group, most of whom buggered the shit out of each other in boarding school.

The average Scot, on the other hand, is a spiky-haired, spandex-clad has-been, clinging desperately to a distant dream of credibility. No matter how insistently he asks, it's safe to say that no, no one thinks he's sexy. On the other hand, the mere sound of a Scottish accent has been known to cause spontaneous orgasm in American women.

Across the Irish Sea, the jolly Papists of Eire are born with the power to fly, and a powerful "sonic scream" that can incapacitate both human beings and animals. For the most part, they use this power to shout at the Northern Irish, who have the temerity to prefer the color orange to green.[10]

The three groups have always hated each other, mostly due to the fact that none of them can understand the others' accents. But whatever their differences, the Scottish, Irish, and English are all incorrigible drunks.

10. One of history's deadliest color wars. *See also: The Camp Waziyatah Massacre of 1984.*

THE WELSH

These vowel-averse Druids are physically indistinguishable from other Britons, but they are also indistinguishable in other ways, as well. Only their names set them apart, like Llewellyn, Caerwyn, Gwyneira, and Tom Jones. And children apparently have a rather unique experience there during the Yuletide season.

CANADIANS

See appendix on **Gays**.

THE FRENCH

It is a little known fact that, despite their romantic culture, the French are born without sex organs. In order to reproduce, they release clouds of spores. So when Serge Gainsbourg told Whitney Houston, "I want to fuck you," on national television, he actually meant that he wanted to ruin her career. Which he did shortly after, by introducing her to Bobby Brown and getting her addicted to crack.

NORDS

Hailing from Scandinavia, Nords are the whitest of the whites. Most people only know them for their incredibly violent death metal, but they are also very blonde. This part of the world is still populated exclusively by the Norse, except for Fin-Land, which is made up mostly of Merpeople.[11]

11. And a handful of thalidomide babies.

MORMONS

The *Village of the Damned*-esque Mormons are a clean, well-mannered race of child-raping cult members. While most Mormons, specifically those in the Latter Day Saints movement, no longer rape children in a culture of forced marriage and incestuous polygamy, some of them still do. They also believe that, any day now, Jesus is going to come and take them away in a giant spaceship.

IT WOULD BE LIBELOUS TO SAY THAT . . .

 Utah Senator Orrin Hatch has close to a dozen prepubescent brides living in a heavily fortified ranch on the outskirts of Provo.

Mormons are more common than you might think, too. When people die in America, the Church of Jesus Christ of Latter Day Saints posthumously converts them to Mormonism without their family's knowledge or consent. Check it out sometime. All of your ancestors have probably been converted to Mormonism, no matter what they believed while they were alive. It saves their souls, and what do your relatives care? They're dead.

AUSTRALIANS

Australia is a post-apocalyptic wasteland, ruled with an iron fist by the evil Lord Humungus. With oil at a premium and no centralized government, the Australians live like beasts, settling their differences

by fighting to the death in large, hemispherical cages. Little is known about what goes on in these so-called "thundered domes," but legend tells that two men enter, but only one man leaves. What happens to the other man is anyone's guess.

Australians also seem to really enjoy barbecuing shrimp.

SOUTH AFRICANS

I know what you're thinking: white Africans? It's true. These Africans are no savage cannibals, though. As an oppressed white minority in southest Africa, they must deal with constant threats to their safety and to their huge caches of diamonds. Perhaps the only thing worse than the racial discrimination they face on a daily basis is sitting through all eighteen minutes of Peter Gabriel's "Biko."

ITALIANS

Italians are only good at two things: plumbing and protecting other people. They are even able to charge a fee for their protection service, it is so useful. Groups of Italians will often join together, in groups so tightly knit they could be families, to better offer their protection to local business owners. Truly, a helpful people.

Physically, Italians are short—comically so—and even the women sport heavily waxed, oversized mustaches. For their work as plumbers they must wear a strict uniform of overalls, white gloves, and matching caps emblazoned with their first initial. But despite what you may have heard about "greasy wops," they are actually terrible cooks. I have sampled extensively from the cuisine of their most famous chef, Salvatore Boyardee, and I've found it consistently bland and unpalatable.

EASTERN EUROPEANS

Eastern Europeans dwell deep beneath the earth in ancient, long-sealed salt mines. Hunched and pale from their years spent underground, they surface only to harvest beets and collude with the Nazis.

They face constant persecution at the hands of unseen, bureaucratic enemies, and due to regional and genetic abnormalities, Eastern Europeans are often transformed into giant bugs while they sleep.

RUSSIANS

Eastern Europe's neighbor to the east, Russia, is even more eastern than Eastern Europe, and the Russians are a hard-used people. It's so bad that in Russia, you don't watch television; television watches you. Moreover, Russians don't ride the bus; the bus rides them. They don't eat dinner; dinner eats them. &c.

ALBINOS

Okay, I take it back: Albinos are actually the whitest whites. They were originally bred by the CIA for stealth in snowy climes, but two of the original test subjects escaped. This pair, Blinky and Bright-eyes, were able to mate, and all albinos living today are directly descended from them.

CONCLUSION

In the end, whites are more to be pitied than feared, whether they be urbane, educated New Englanders, or backward, borderline-retarded outlanders. They are bubbling, overflowing cauldrons of racial hatred, it is true, but most of that hatred is directed inward, and takes the

form of guilt. And, really, haven't they suffered enough?

FURTHER READING

If you're interested in learning more about white people, here are some suggestions for further reading:

Duke, David. *My Awakening*. Free Speech Books, 1998.

Hitler, Adolf. *Mein Kampf*. Franz Eher, 1927.

Keane, Bil. *The Family Circus: Dolly Hit Me Back!* Fawcett, 1985.

~⁓⁓~

INDIANS (AND INJUNS)

A PRACTICAL GUIDE TO REDSKINS

When Christopher Columbus discovered America in 1492, he thought he had reached India, and so he called the natives "Indians." These were the people we know today as Injuns, but Columbus wasn't entirely wrong. Despite his incompetence as a navigator, he was an astute racial scholar. He saw the red skin and oriental features of the savages and immediately recognized them as ethnically subcontinental.

Injuns are sometimes referred to as "Native Americans," because they are native to the Americas, like the Protestants, but they originally come from India. At one point, the Indian subcontinent was physically connected to North America as part of the super-continent,

Pangaea.[1] If you look at a map of the world, you can actually see where the two landmasses fit together, before the tectonic shift.

Fig. 1. Pangaea

When Pangaea broke apart in the twelfth century, the peoples of India were split in two. Half remained in southern Asia, where their population expanded exponentially, while the other half were trapped in what became the Americas, where, for some unknown reason, their numbers dropped precipitously over the course of the last 400 years. Clearly, Hindoos are more suited to the tropical climate of their origin.

The similarities between the two groups are undeniable, and it's not just their reddish-brown skin, coarse black hair, and frequent nudity. Indians and Injuns are both good with herbs and potions, both worship multiple pagan gods, and both speak the same language, as far as I can tell.

They are, genetically, the same race, but the two groups have been separated for so long that some dissimilarities have developed, as well. The evolutionary adaptation of Indians and Injuns has diverged, both physically and culturally, like two geographically disparate populations of finches.

Fig. 2. Can you tell which is which?

1. Literally, "super continent."

In this chapter, we will look at each in turn, with an eye to their shared traits, as well as the dissimilarities that define them.

INDIANS

The Indian race in Asia is divided chiefly among India, Pakistan, Bangladesh, and Sri Lanka, the region we call "Hindoostan." Once known only as a boundless natural reserve of teakwood, saffron, and Darjeeling tea, Hindoostan is now home to billions of the world's dirtiest people.

Imagine for a moment, if you will, that the Revolutionary War had never happened, that America had remained a colony of Great Britain until 1947, and that U.S. citizens had been subject to the tyrannical laws and disastrous economic policies of the British during that period. Not that this bears on the Indian situation in any way. I just think it's an interesting counterfactual exercise, like, "what if the Germans had won World War II, and Hitler had married Marilyn Monroe?"[2]

Sixty years ago, India declared its independence from Great Britain, and ever since then its people have lived a savage, overcrowded existence, barely able to muster the strength or civility for a friendly game of cricket or an afternoon tea. There is much good in the Hindoo race, but now that they are no longer coddled under the protective thumb of the British Empire, it appears that they have returned to their state of nature.[3]

2. Perhaps his stern, authoritarian presence could have averted catastrophe and she might still be with us today.

3. And, like life in the state of nature, Indians are nasty, brutish, and small in stature.

CULTURE

After biting the hand that had fed them for almost a century, Indians almost immediately reverted to their ancient tribal practices and mysterious native rites. The modern Hindoos, or "Coolies," worship an ever-growing pantheon of grotesque, many-armed deities: genderless, impossibly bosomed gods who practice wanton sexual debauchery in a dizzying array of positions and combinations.

The base, pansexual behavior of their gods and goddesses may explain a similar inclination in the Hindoos themselves. As any book of Indian art will tell you, they are a race of lithe, flexible perverts. The most popular pastime of the Hindoo race, after choreographed dance numbers, is autoerotic asphyxiation, and the two are often performed in tandem.

THINGS INDIANS HAVE STOLEN
FROM THE BLACKS

1. Bhangra
2. Pantheism
3. Turbans
4. Taxi medallions

Nor are their strange customs merely sexual in nature. Every year, hundreds of millions of scantily clad Indians voluntarily leap into the world's most polluted river, the Ganges, in order to complete the sacred Hindoo rite of "contracting hepatitis C."[4] They also believe that

4. Indian immigrants in America, unable to reach the Ganges, are able to get the same effect from the Hudson River.

cows are somehow sacred, an unusual idea that was famously inspired by the signature catchphrase of Yankees announcer Phil Rizzuto.[5]

The Hindoo political system is just as obscure. Since the dissolution of the benevolent British *Raj*, India has been ruled by a succession of Gandhis, from Indira to Rajiv to Sonia, each one a clone of the original Gandhi: Mahatma. Whenever a ruler dies, Mahatma Gandhi is cloned from the DNA in his severed head, which has been cryogenically frozen and stored in the Disney vault.

THE CASTE SYSTEM

Unlike Great Britain, Indian society is divided into a rigid and exclusionary class system. Every Hindoo is a member of one of five castes, among which there is no mixing; those who are found intermingling between castes are sent into the Forbidden Zone, from which there is no return. If the radiation does not kill them there, they will surely waste away in its vast emptiness, populated only by the detritus of a once-great society.

*At the top of this social order is the **Brahmin** caste, which is composed of scholars and priests. India is one of the few countries in the world where smart, educated people are looked up to by their social inferiors. In America, they are forced to live on meager stipends and research grants, and claw each others' eyes out competing for the slightest hint of job security.*

*Below the Brahmins are the **Kshatriyas**, the aristocrats and rulers, who govern the corporeal lives of men, just as the Brahmins gov-*

5. He introduced it to the natives on one of his many spiritual pilgrimages to the Orient. In some regions of Bangladesh, Rizzuto was worshipped as a living god.

ern their spiritual lives. Being a Kshatriya is the Indian equivalent of being in Skull and Bones, or having gone to Andover.

*The **Vaishyas** are the merchants and landowners of Indian society. They control much of the country's wealth, and are some of its most influential private citizens, while below them, **Shudras** are its farmers and its manual laborers. Some of the most popular sitcoms in India are about fat, shudra slobs who are married to improbably hot, capable women.*[6]

*At the very bottom of the Hindoo caste system are the **Untouchables**, sometimes called "**Dalits.**"*[7] *The Dalits are looked down upon by all members of society, and are forced to do India's most degrading, menial labor. In Hindoostan, sewage workers, pharmaceutical test subjects, and fluffers are invariably Dalits.*

As John Lennon said, "Dalits are the nigger of the world."

Unfortunately, there is no potential for upward mobility in Indian society. In the classic Indian children's story "The Little Match Girl," the protagonist is stoned to death for daring to speak to a Brahmin.

Hindoo society and customs may seem odd, but there is also method in their madness. The Hindoo public transportation system, for example, is a model of efficiency and energy conservation. As scientists, they have developed a wide range of spicy, delicious laxatives, and as entrepreneurs they have made millions by convincing American women to stretch together in a sweaty room. And their tradition

6. Every Thursday, millions of Hindoos tune in to see the latest misadventures of *The Raj of Mumbai.*
7. Two of the most famous Dalits are actors Sean Connery and Kevin Costner.

Fig. 3. The Indian public transportation system

of arranged marriages makes Indians the envy of Jewish mothers all over the world.

The Hindoo race has many strange customs and proclivities, it is true, but there is great potential there as well. If given the proper education and hygiene, they can be exemplary members of civilized society, as many Indian-Americans have shown.

According to U.S. law, Indians are ethnically Asian,[8] but my studies have revealed in them none of the usual Asian deviousness. In fact, they show no desire to invade America whatsoever, and their dusky skin diminishes the yellow aggression we often see in Orientals.

THE GLOBAL INDIAN

Indians have spread all over the world, even here to America, where they own and operate our convenience stores, drive our cabs, and answer our tech-support questions from local call centers. It is a credit to their race that they are able to apply their training as surgeons, lawyers, and scholars to these challenging new vocations. It is also a

8. As determined by the 1923 Supreme Court case *United States v. Bhagat Singh Thind*. The Supreme Court has always been the highest ethnographic body in the land.

testament to the Indians' humility and resilience that they have been able to overcome their ancient feud with our American cowboys.

There have been setbacks, and to avoid having their stores vandalized they should really do more to distinguish themselves from Arabs, but the Hindoos are among our most successful immigrants.

INDIANS IN THE MEDIA

Many movies, television shows, and radio serials feature Indian supporting characters, but not all of them are positive or fair. Real Hindoos are nothing like the crass, racist stereotypes perpetuated by Hank Azaria and his voice-actor cronies. The following are just a few positive examples of Indians in the media, but each has much to teach us about his culture.

- Ben Kingsley — *A courageous Indian actor, he shows the power of nonviolent resistance in his autobiographical movie,* Gandhi.
- Dhalsim — *One of the brave warriors who tested their mettle against Vega, Sagat, Balrog, and M. Bison in the* Street Fighter *competition, he demonstrates that Indians can stretch their limbs to impossible lengths, and breathe fire.*
- Tony Shalhoub — *An obsessive-compulsive detective in San Francisco, he helps his adopted homeland by solving crimes.*
- Kaavya Viswanathan — *The critically acclaimed author of* How Opal Mehta Got Kissed, Got Wild, and Got a

Life, *she is an inspiration to young female writers everywhere.*

- Great Tiger — *A successful boxer and magician, his one weakness is that he telegraphs his moves via a flashing crystal in his turban.*
- The Parade of Hot Indian Women on BBC News — *Erudite, intelligent journalists, they teach us that Indian women can have English accents, which makes them even hotter.*

Figures like these teach us that the Hindoos are a nonviolent, magical, fastidious, stretchy, and pugnacious people.

Indians are becoming more and more prominent in Western popular media, but few people realize that they also make their own movies—thousands of them every day. The Hindoo movie industry is known as "Bollywood," which is a pun on America's Hollywood,[9] but major Bollywood movies, unlike American ones, are empty spectacles. Still, anyone interested in how native Indians interact would be well-served by picking up a title like Dil Ka Rishta *or* Lagaan, *to learn the appropriate dances and songs to perform when you meet with an Indian acquaintance or business partner.*

9. Not to be confused with Bollywood the theme park, in Mumbai. That is a pun on Dollywood.

Indians may seem mysterious, and it is true that their customs are strange and savage, but given the opportunity they are also hard-working and helpful, and make excellent manservants and adventure sidekicks.

They are, however, hindered by the rifts that divide them as a race. The peoples of India and Pakistan seem unable to coexist peacefully, even though they are all the same race and religion. A Hindoo is a Hindoo, whether he comes from India, where they worship Brahma the creator, Vishnu the preserver, and Shiva the destroyer, or Pakistan, where they also worship those same three gods.

Much of the animosity seems to stem from a dispute over who owns the rights to "Kashmir," a song from the Led Zeppelin album *Physical Graffiti*. In any case, it probably won't get out of hand, as long as neither country acquires nuclear technology.

INJUNS

Like their ethnic brothers, the Indians, Injuns have a dark, reddish-brown skin, and a deep connection to the spiritual world, but the physical and dispositional similarities between the two populations are sometimes obscured by their cultural differences.

While Indians have made an effort to globalize and embrace the Western world, Injuns rarely interact with real Americans, instead choosing to remain sequestered on their reservations. I have never personally understood this sort of self-segregation, like black fraternities or Gypsy caravans. These races would be better served by letting their own cultures disappear entirely, and assimilating into ours.

When Injuns do leave their reservations, it is only to purchase alco-

hol or to attack defenseless wagon trains with their primitive weapons. Conversely, white men rarely visit these reservations, except to spend millions of dollars every day on gambling, hotels, and Michael McDonald concerts.

CULTURE

Injun culture has long been opaque to the common man, because the Injuns tend to keep to themselves. They seem almost beaten down for some reason. The U.S. government has done everything it can to reach out to them, donating millions of blankets and literally hundreds of acres of land, but nothing seems to help.

The Injuns most of us are familiar with are violent and anti-American, like Leonard Peltier and Injun Joe. They use their spears, arrows, and thundersticks to attack Western settlers and FBI agents, but these are only a few, angry souls. Most Injuns are too dazed by drug use and alcoholism to do anything more than slump down on their horses in resignation.

Firewater addiction is a part of Injun culture, just like rain dances and tom-tom drums, but Injuns have also begun abusing psychotropic drugs such as peyote and "wacky tobacky," which they smoke in long, wooden peace pipes. If you're won-dering why this sort of lawlessness is

Fig. 4. "End of the Trail," by James Earl Fraser

permitted to go on, it's because they claim that the peyote is part of their religious rituals. They may have fooled the government, but I know for a fact that there is nothing in the Bible about hallucinogens.

This substance abuse has, predictably, kept Injuns from achieving any kind of worldly success. It is no accident that there are so few prominent Injuns working in the public sector or media. They are terrible actors, as Steven Seagal's *On Deadly Ground* demonstrates, and even worse musicians.[10] Some have even failed at both pursuits, like the Injun from the Village People. One notable exception to this tradition of failure is the Land O'Lakes girl, who is famous for both her beauty and her talent.[11]

This lackluster record of achievement extends to other arenas as well. They hunted buffalo for centuries, but failed to kill them all. It only took European settlers fifty years to take care of that. As barbers, they are imprecise and careless, often removing all of the client's hair in one stroke, along with the skin it was attached to. And the writing of Sherman Alexie rarely elevates itself above the modest standards of ethnic literature.

It probably won't surprise you, then, that the Injuns are also inveterate litterers. It is the worst kind of hypocrisy for them to shed a single, poignant tear every time we throw a bag of trash at their feet, while they are out littering the entire country with their detritus. You can hardly go for a walk in the forest without tripping over one of their arrowheads or a string of their primitive beads.

There is some hope for America's terminally unemployable braves and squaws, in the form of casinos. The United States lets Injuns build casinos for religious reasons, and they provide a steady stream of croupier and pit-boss jobs for local tribe members. Of course, a casino might not provide the best environment for such addictive personalities, but I'm sure they will bring only good things to the Injun people.

10. Buffy Sainte-Marie
11. As a butter holder.

If there is one place where drug-addled outcasts can succeed, it is the fashion world, and the Injuns are no exception. Their innovations in leather fringe remain popular among '70s revivalists, and moccasins, which they invented, are a great way for middle-aged women to keep their feet warm around the house. But perhaps their biggest fashion statement is the mohawk.

First worn by the Mohawk tribe on the East Coast,[12] this unusual haircut has inspired luminaries from Mr. T to Dexter Manley to thousands of suburban white teenagers without strong parental figures. Not to mention the devotees of the faux-hawk, or Sanjaya Malakar's iconic pony-hawk.

One thing you might not realize is that Injuns also invented the Baby Björn,[13] a type of infant receptacle that has become hugely popular with wealthy, condescending parents everywhere. It's actually not that surprising, if you think about it. Children have always loved Injuns, from their silly little kachina dolls, to their big, goofy totem poles. Injun dream catchers are affixed to many a bunk bed, and I don't know a red-blooded American child who hasn't dressed up in a funny outfit, put on some "war paint" and whoop-whoop-whooped it up in the backyard with his friends. It's all good fun, and they're learning about history, too.

Fig. 5. Punk rock

12. Injuns divide themselves into tribes, like the Dahlonega and the Pygmy, but only for tax purposes.

13. Most people assume that they were created by the Swedes.

COMMON STEREOTYPES

Despite what you might expect, many of the stereotypes about Injuns are actually quite positive. In America, these flattering stereotypes vary by region, and tend to speak more to the Injuns' proud past than their troubled present.

In the American South, for example, there is the stereotype of the **Brave**, which is found mostly in Georgia. The Brave is a courageous, feather-coiffed competitor, known for his war songs and his mighty tomahawk chop. Further south, in Tallahassee, the prevailing view of Injuns is of the **Seminole**, a spear-wielding young Injun on horseback, who is known for leading cheers in front of large crowds, and for owning the hotel where Anna Nicole Smith died.

In the exurbs of the nation's capital, people tend to think of the **Redskin**, a slightly more cartoonish figure. The Redskin typifies the big-nosed, rain-dancing stereotype of Injuns, but he is also traditionally very strong on defense, and pioneered the use of the counter trey.

Midwesterners are more familiar with the generic Cleveland **Injun**, a very red man with an extremely wide smile, known for beating on tom-tom drums and, as in the case of famous Injun Willie Mays Hayes, nailing a pair of gloves to the wall for every base he steals. Down in Missouri, the most dominant image is that of the Injun **Chief**, a proud leader of men with a flashy offense and a tradition of choking in the postseason.

Stereotypes like these, that paint a flattering portrait of Injuns, are an encouraging counterpoint to the minstrelsy that we see in other races. It is important to foster such positive stereotypes at every level, and to pass them on to future generations. California teens, for example, are taught an important lesson in tolerance from the wise, powerful **Big Chief Wampum Stomp'em**, the mascot of Andrew Jackson High School in Bakersfield.

HISTORY

One cannot truly understand the Injun without understanding his history, and that history is one of great hardship. For many years, Injuns lived a harsh, uncivilized existence, barely clothed and surviving off whatever they could scrounge from the forest floor.

These ancient Injuns frequently killed each other over land or food, and the evidence of their brutality is still being discovered. Only forty years ago, thousands of human hearts were discovered, buried for centuries beneath the ground in Wounded Knee, South Dakota. The Injuns would have gone on this way indefinitely, living in a savage equilibrium with nature, if it had not been for the arrival of the Americans in the fifteenth century.

When the Americans arrived from Europe, they brought with them horses and guns, but more importantly, they brought civilization. In the form of horses and guns.

At the time, Injuns lived in every part of the country, rather than just the small, rural reservations to which they were entitled. It took many years, but with the help of the Bureau of Injun Affairs, the government was able to place them in their proper habitats.

It is not a commonly known stereotype, but Injuns are actually excellent negotiators. They sold the island of Manhattan—which they didn't even own—to a bunch of gullible Dutch tourists for $24.[14] The tribe tried to throw in the Brooklyn Bridge as well, but the Netherlanders weren't dumb enough to fall for that old trick, especially since the bridge wouldn't be built for more than 200 years.

Injuns also negotiated a series of highly unfair treaties with the U.S. government. The treaties were so imbalanced in favor of the

14. Adjusted for inflation, $24 in seventeenth-century money is the modern equivalent of $600 trillion.

Injuns that we repeatedly had to break them just to create a level playing field. The United States really got corn-holed by some of those agreements, or, as the Injuns say, "maize-holed."

Luckily, it didn't take much convincing from that great diplomat, Andrew Jackson, to herd the Injuns back onto their reservations, where they belonged. When they finally started the long hike to their new homes, some Injuns even wept for joy.

Fig. 6. The Great Compromiser

There were Injuns in Mexico and the lower Americas, too, but they didn't cause nearly as much trouble. These were groups like the Aztecs, the Toltecs, the Olmecs, the Incas, and the Jew-hating Mayans.[15] When they weren't performing human sacrifices, building steppe pyramids, or worshipping the feathered serpent, Quetzalcoatl, these southern Injuns were out getting knocked up by Hispanics. That's why much of the lower Americas are today overrun by a *mole*-eating race of half-breed *mestizos*.

CONCLUSION

There are many superficial differences between Indians and Injuns. From their manners of dress to their attitudes, they seem at first glance to be entirely different races. It is only through the trained lens of

15. Their anti-Semitism is discussed in more depth in the movie *Apocalypto*.

science that we have found these two groups to be part of the same, overarching ethnicity.

Now that we know that they are members of the same race, it is easy to see the overwhelming similarities between them. They are unmistakably alike in their physical traits, such as the redness of their skin and the wiry agility of their frames, as well as

Fig. 7. Kinky

many of their less tangible qualities. For example, both groups make excellent sidekicks. Hadji was an able partner to Race Bannon, while the Injun Tonto served as the Lone Ranger's sadomasochistic submissive for many years.

My theory is that all of the differences between the two groups can be explained by their different habitats and cultural influences over the last few centuries. The Hindoos benefited for many years from the civilizing influence of their English rulers, and it shows. Not many races wear white slacks, or drink that much (non-hallucinogenic) tea. Despite their savage tendencies, this is clearly a people that has benefited from British rule, and their current success bears this out.

The Hindoos eventually rejected their benevolent British overseers, but only after decades of idyllic life in the Empire. Injuns, on the other hand, never had this advantage. They rebelled against American culture from the start, and, when they failed, they simply removed themselves from modern life altogether. It is only in recent years that Injuns have made any attempt to integrate into American society, and only time will tell if they will be successful.

If you removed their cultural and geographical influences, I believe

that the apparent dissimilarities between Indians and Injuns would disappear. As it stands, Hindoos and Injuns are far more alike than we had previously realized. Let us return to our earlier diagram.

At first glance, the styles of dress don't look anything alike, but if you look closer, you can see that the asymmetries are almost entirely the result of differences in habitat. The Hindoo wears a loose-

Fig. 8

fitting cotton wrap, while the Injun wears a warmer leather garb, but the two garments are remarkably alike. It is only the material that differs: leather for the chillier climes of North America, and cotton for tropical Hindoostan. Likewise, the Hindoo wears a turban and the Injun wears a feathered headdress, but if you think about it, both are just covering their heads with silly-looking hats. These apparent, superficial differences belie a much deeper, ethnographic sameness.

History and society may have treated them differently, but the Indians and the Injuns are, in fact, one and the same. And, perhaps one day, both will accept the full benefit of Western rule.

It is important to remember that, while they may live filthy, sub-human existences, ungraced by the rule of law, Indians and Injuns are also wise in their own way. They are proud, brown peoples, with a deep, mystical understanding of both the spirit and the natural world. We can learn a lot from their vision quests[16] and yoga trances.

There is a nobility to these savages that we must not ignore.

16. In these vision quests, Injuns push themselves to follow their dream of wrestling for the state championship.

FURTHER READING

If you're interested in learning more about the Indian and Injun people, here are some suggestions for further reading:

Thomas, Robert B. "Sunrise and Sunset Calendar," in *The Farmer's Almanack of the British Empire*. Little Brown & Company, 1947.

Banks, Lynne Reid. *The Injun in the Cupboard*. Doubleday, 1980.

BLACKS

A PRACTICAL GUIDE TO MELANIN

B lacks have had it pretty easy. They are beloved around the world, they are captains of industry, and they have adorable babies. They have been so successful that other races slavishly imitate their every trend and behavioral tic, from cornrows to gun violence to poor grammar.

This worldly success is directly related to their lives of relative ease, and vice versa. With god-like status in the eyes of their fellow men, blacks haven't had to deal with horrors like reverse racism or white slavery. That freedom has, in turn, given them the affluence and leisure time to become virtuoso athletes, rhymesmiths, and dominoes

players. There was even a black president of the United States of America on the television show *24*.[1]

Some people have claimed that it's because blacks are naturally superior to the other races. They say that their genetic material has made them smarter, more civilized, and harder working. Some even believe that black, or "colored" people keep better time than other ethnicities, but that is all bunk. The black's overwhelming success in business, art, and politics is due to cultural—not genetic—factors.

Only their athletic success is due to innate physical superiority, a fact that is controversial for some reason. Jimmy the Greek explained it best when he said, "The black is a better athlete to begin with because he has been bred to be that way."

Yes, life has been sweet for the blacks in this country, but who is the Black? For starters, he is a generous friend, known for both his wisdom and his kindness. You might have

Fig. 1. Noted racial scholar Jimmy T.G. Snyder

heard the myth of the "angry black man," but that is actually nothing more than an etymological holdover from the Anglo-Saxon word "angrie," which means "well-respected."

Above all the black is a family man, known for his big heart and his even bigger appetites. A mere twelve ounces of malted liquor is enough for most people, but blacks require more than three times that amount. And while non-blacks will frequently wear just one or two

1. David Palmer was perhaps our greatest fictional president.

Fig. 2

pieces of jewelry, black people drape themselves in as much "bling" as possible, even if it sometimes interferes with their crime-fighting duties.

These outsized attitudes also hold true for intercourse, which is why blacks have such large families, despite being neither Catholic nor poor. They are especially known for their extensive networks of nieces and nephews.

These large families are a constant source of support, especially when the father sticks around, and are a large part of why blacks have been so successful in this country. In

Fig. 3. Benjamin Hawthorne, center, with his three nephews and two nieces

fact, they have only one natural enemy, other than ashiness: they are beset on all sides by the violent romantic desires of wild, savage white women. These sexually predatory *succubae* will stop at nothing to get what they want, and what they want is black babies.

Fig. 4. Jemima Anne Porter, center, with just a few of her many nieces and nephews

The offspring of mixed-race couplings are, of course, black, because it only takes one drop of black blood to make someone black. Such lighter-skinned black people are sometimes referred to as mulattoes, after the Dairy Queen drink, the "MooLatté®."[2]

In order to evade all these unwanted advances, black men are often forced to disguise themselves as fat, older women. It's not uncommon to see a young man disguising himself as a big momma or a mad black woman or a grandmamma.

2. The MooLatté® mixes chocolate and vanilla flavors into a delicious, light-brown coffee drink. You can also try their banana shake, the High Yellow Breezer®, or their double-fudge shake, Uncle Yum's Cabin®.

*THINGS BLACKS HAVE STOLEN
FROM THE BLACKS*

1. Wallets
2. Starter™ Jackets
3. Air Jordans™
4. PSPs

There is a long history of cinema, books, and music that deal with the black man's sexual fears and neuroses. His worst nightmare is played to great effect in the movie *Traffic*, when a large black man is graphically preyed upon by a comatose, drug-addled white teenager. This sick seduction is performed even more subtly and artfully in movies like *Mandingo* and Todd Solondz's *Storytelling*.[3] It's a tradition in popular culture that goes back to noted civil rights activist and filmmaker D.W. Griffith, and was carried on by authors like Herman Talmadge and songsmiths like Hartford A. Pennywhistle, who topped the charts in 1928 with his ragtime hit, "N-words Shan't Be Plowing My Daughter (No Sir)."

Until recently, there were laws to prevent such miscegenation. All over the country, legislatures leapt at the chance to protect the black man from the wiles of his sexy, white tormentors. Unfortunately, the Warren court undid all that good with a few misguided rulings.

After all, it's not always easy on the top. As John Lennon said, "Blacks are the nigger of the world."

In 1967, in the ironically named case of *Loving v. Virginia*, the all-

3. Unfortunately, for most audiences this moving scene is hidden behind a large red box.

white Supreme Court struck down Virginia's Racial Integrity Act of 1924. Based on the equal protection clause of the Fourteenth Amendment, Chief Justice Earl Warren ruled that laws against intermarriage were unconstitutional, because "Marriage is one of the 'basic civil rights of man,' fundamental to our very existence and survival." Presciently adding, "unless they're fags."

Despite the ruling, Alabama bravely held onto its anti-miscegenation laws until 2000. When the state finally bowed to national pressure, it removed the black man's final protection against lascivious white women.

Alabama held out so long because it has always been a friend to the blacks. It even let the Reverend Dr. Martin Luther King, Jr., stage one of his good-time revival marches in its largest city, back in 1963.[4] Then, when he needed a rest and a place to compose a nice, long letter, the Birmingham police allowed King to use one of their jail cells and gave him a whole roll of toilet paper to write it on.

Of course, the South has long been a shining beacon of racial harmony in the United States. Let's look back now at the history of blacks, from the dawn of man to the present day.

A TIMELINE OF BLACK HISTORY

2650 B.C. Egyptians build the great pyramids and lead the world in intellectual thought. 5,000 years later, still known for those same pyramids.

1200 B.C. Egypt is ruled by the Pharaoh Tutankhamen, who generously leaves behind lots of cool stuff for us to find.

4. It was a hot spring day, but the local firefighters were nice enough to use their hoses to cool down the marchers.

51 B.C. Cleopatra rises to power in Egypt, nearly bankrupting 20th Century Fox in the process.

300 A.D. Aksum rises in modern-day Ethiopia as a Christian kingdom. Creates first black Jesus on record.

600 Ghana established as a trading empire.

610 Advent of Islam. Prophet Mohammed immediately stoned for being a visual representation of himself.

740 Moors spend semester in Spain.

1230 Sundiata Keita establishes Mali empire. His mother was an ugly, hunchbacked woman named Sogolon, or "buffalo woman." Fortunately for him, the "yo mama" joke wouldn't be invented for more than 700 years.

1307 Mansa Musa takes throne of Mali empire. The name "Mansa Musa" is all that most people will retain from African history segment in junior high.

1441–1865 Nothing of any significance happens to black people.

1865 Affirmative action created.

1865–1877 Blacks briefly hold elected office in the South, accomplish everything they set out to do, and thus never need to serve again.

1867 Hillman College founded in Washington, D.C.

1870 Fifteenth Amendment passed, giving all black men the right to vote for white people.

1881 Tuskegee Institute founded. Will educate many prominent black leaders, as well as Lionel Richie.

1895　　Booker T. Washington gives his famous "Atlanta Compromise" speech. Unfortunately, due to racial restrictions in Atlanta, he is forced to compromise and give the speech in nearby Decatur.

1896　　The Supreme Court rules in the case of *Plessy v. Ferguson*. The case is won by either Plessy or Ferguson.

1899　　Scott Joplin writes his "Maple Leaf Rag." His racial background comes as a shock to many who had assumed that anyone who would write such a vanilla ragtime piano melody must be white.

1901　　Booker T. Washington has dinner at the White House with President Theodore Roosevelt. White House correspondent Fuzzy Zoeller can only speculate as to the menu that evening.

1903　　W.E.B. DuBois suggests the idea of a "Talented Tenth" for the black community. That talent? Cunnilingus.

1905　　Madame C.J. Walker becomes America's first black female millionaire after inventing a method of straightening curly hair. She doubles her money twice over when she successfully invents a skin-bleaching treatment, as well.

1909　　The NAACP is founded, with a full name that white people will be uncomfortable saying for centuries to come.

1914　　Marcus Garvey founds the Universal Negro Improvement Association, dedicated partly to the improvement of Negroes, but mostly to the wearing of funny hats.

1914　　George Washington Carver announces the success of his experiments with peanuts. This fact is all that most

people will retain from African American history segment in junior high.

1916–1970 The Great Migration. Tens of thousands of blacks move from the rural South to the urban centers of the North for some reason.

1917–1919 Black soldiers serve heroically as fodder for German cannons.

1920 Negro baseball leagues founded. Players wear cool "throwback" jerseys.

1925 Brotherhood of Sleeping Car Porters founded, the first successful black trade union. Slogan "It's sho' 'nuff possible" fails to catch on as well as Cesar Chavez's "Si se puede."

1932–1972 The U.S. Public Health Service studies effects of untreated syphilis in black men in Tuskegee, Alabama. The experiments are shut down, in 1972, after the passage of the controversial "Rural Blacks Are Human Beings" Act.

1936 Jesse Owens wins four gold medals at the summer Olympics in Berlin. The German team fares much better two years later at the biathlon, in which a competitor skis down a slope and then randomly shoots people from his balcony.

1937 Zora Neale Hurston publishes *Their Eyes Were Watching God*, giving future high school students some seriously hot, steamy homework.

1941 Tuskegee Airmen founded, largely syphilis-free.

1945 *Ebony* magazine founded, providing thousands of dentists with racially diverse reading material for their waiting rooms.

1947 Jackie Robinson becomes first black player in Major League Baseball, for the Brooklyn Dodgers. The team is so named

for their skill at avoiding the projectiles hurled at them from the stands when they play.

1950 Chuck Cooper, of the Boston Celtics, becomes first black professional basketball player. *(See 2005 – Darko Milicic becomes last white professional basketball player.)*

1954 The Supreme Court eliminates school segregation with its ruling in *Brown v. Board of Education of Topeka.* Segregation then immediately reinstated after Earl Warren's daughter impregnated by a black classmate.

1955 Rosa Parks refuses to give up her bus seat to a white person. The one-legged pregnant woman is forced to sit in the aisle.

1956 The Sudan gains its independence. The British didn't want it anymore, anyway.

1957 The National Guard is dispatched to Little Rock, Arkansas, to force Governor Orville Faubus to allow integration. The operation is temporarily derailed when the Guardsmen can't stop laughing at the name "Orville Faubus."

1958–1977 Bit by bit, most of the rest of Africa gains its independence from the colonial powers of Europe.

1962 Nelson Mandela imprisoned because he is black, and for no other reason.

1963 The Reverend Dr. Martin Luther King, Jr., speaks at August's March on Washington. Louis Farrakhan bitterly disputes the official count, which puts the number of attendees at only about 200,000.

1965 Watts riots the worst riots ever to occur in Los Angeles (at the time).

1966 Bobby Seale and Huey Newton found Black Panthers in effort to create easily co-optable revolutionary iconography.

1966 Kwanzaa created by Ron Karenga as alternative to Christmas for black people, because if there's one thing that black people hate, it's receiving presents.

1967 Thurgood Marshall appointed to the Supreme Court, despite a scandal in which he allegedly placed a pubic hair on a female colleague's can of Diet Coke.

1968 Martin Luther King, Jr., assassinated by James Earl Ray, giving radio's "Greaseman" a *hi-larious* idea for a joke.

1974 Hank Aaron, totally cranked on HGH and anabolic steroids, hits his record 715th career home run.

1975 Arthur Ashe wins singles title at Wimbledon, proving that blacks can beat white people at *any* sport.

1977 Alex Haley's *Roots* adapted for TV. Geordi LaForge plays it kind of dark.

1980 Zimbabwe gains its independence from Great Britain. Seriously. 1980.

1982 Michael Jackson releases *Thriller. (See also White History Timeline, 1991 – Michael Jackson releases* Dangerous.*)*

1983 Jesse Jackson runs for president on an all-rhyming platform.

1985–1990 Crack.

1990 Nelson Mandela released from prison, finally vindicating the efforts of The Specials.

1991 Motorist Rodney King suffers eleven skull fractures, broken bones and teeth, and permanent brain damage, when he trips and falls onto the batons of four Los Angeles police officers.

1992 The four policemen, including Sergeant Stacey Koon, whose last name ironically describes one of his least favorite things, are acquitted on all charges. In response, local blacks decide to burn down their own neighborhoods.

1993 Cornel West publishes the seminal work *Race Matters* as part of a decade-long audition for a speaking part in one of the *Matrix* sequels.

1994 Nelson Mandela elected president of South Africa. The Specials kick themselves for not writing a song urging people to elect Nelson Mandela, elect, elect, elect Nelson Mandela.

Courtesy Office of Communications, Princeton University

1995 O. J. Simpson acquitted of murdering his wife, inciting three days of rioting among LA's white population.

1997 Tiger Woods wins the Masters golf tournament, hammering home the point made by Arthur Ashe two decades earlier.

2001 Colin Powell appointed Secretary of State. Despite initial misgivings, position involves relatively little typing or filing.

2005 Condoleezza Rice appointed Secretary of State. Immediately put to work transcribing Donald Rumsfeld's dictation.

2008 Barack Obama discredited somehow.

A FEW COMMON STEREOTYPES

Blacks have been relatively free from institutional discrimination in this country, except for a brief period in the 1970s, when they were shamelessly blaxploited by Hollywood. But that doesn't mean that stereotypes about them don't exist, both good and bad.

Perhaps the most common black stereotype today is the **Gangsta**. This character is a tough, streetwise n-word who frequently commits murder crimes.[5] He is recognizable by his 9mm handgun and the impractical, sideways grip with which he holds it. The prevalence of this stereotype may explain why some people are actually afraid of black men.

While there are some actual "gangstas"—mostly in the "hood"—the stereotype's popularity is mostly due to its widespread popularity within the black community itself. In an unusual trend of intra-racial minstrelsy, many black men pretend to be gangstas by wearing comically baggy clothing and using poor grammar.

Fig. 5. Bert Williams in blacker face

The gangsta should not be confused with the **Pimp**, someone who exploits and abuses women for a living. And *what* a living! The pimp is justly celebrated in black culture for his flamboyant style, his outlaw status, and of course for his serial exploitation and abuse of vulnerable and drug-addicted women.

Criminality is not entirely foreign to the African American community, but it is mostly limited to the **Trickster**, a fleet-footed mischief-maker. This lapine figure is known for getting himself out of jams with his quick wit and high vertical leap.[6]

The best way to avoid being victimized by one of these rascals is to

5. In the future, these will be known as M.D.K.s, or "Murder Death Kills."

6. A prominent example of the trickster archetype is the modern-day **Nigerian**, who uses e-mails to convince stupid people to send him money.

trap him using a baby doll made out of tar and turpentine. The doll is so sticky that the tricky n-word won't be able to free himself, and you can retrieve your valuables from him at your leisure.

Some people take offense at the notion that black people are naturally inclined to larceny, but I believe science is on my side with this one. I'm reminded of a scene I witnessed not too long ago. A middle-aged white woman was eating at a fast-food establishment with her young son (also white), when the boy noticed a black

Fig. 6. A black man in evening dress

man eating alone nearby. "Look, mommy," he cried, "a robber!"

As my good friend Noam Chomsky would say, this child was born with an innate recognition of the form $b = r$, where b is "black people" and r is "robbers." On being confronted with a relevant, real-world situation, he was able to apply this form to the problem at hand. You certainly can't *teach* that kind of racism.

The stereotype of the lovable **Crackhead** is less prevalent now than it was in the late 1980s, when it was introduced to urban neighborhoods by the CIA. And as stereotypes go, it certainly caught on. The crackhead is a modern-day version of the **Sambo**, a singing, dancing, laughing n-word. The sambo is perpetually happy and helpful, and speaks with an unusual cadence, much like that of George Lucas's unforgettable alien, Jar Jar Binks.[7]

In fact, there was only ever one actual sambo: Rufus Allen Sambo, a mentally retarded black man who lived in the Reconstruction South.

7. A delightful character. He single-handedly saves the otherwise subpar *Phantom Menace*.

Fig. 7 Hoptoit McNegropants in his hit comedy, The Gamboling Ghost

Unemployable because of his disability, he spent all day, every day, dancing and singing nonsense songs on the street corners of Charleston. The stereotype has persisted so long because of its popularity in film and television, and it was employed for comic effect by characters like Uncle Remus, Rochester, Stepin Fetchit, and Hoptoit McNegropants.

Despite the hilarious antics of the actors who have played the character, I think this is one stereotype we can put to bed for good. No one views black people as mere entertainment anymore.

BLACKS AROUND THE WORLD

Stereotypes don't just exist in America. African Americans across the globe are all basically the same,[8] whether they be European African Americans, Caribbean African Americans, or African African Americans, but there are different stereotypes about each of them.

*Despite what you may have heard about "marijuana cigarettes" and "not bathing," **Jamaicans** are no different from blacks anywhere else. Legend has it that the stereotype of the dreadlocked, music-making Jamaican was created out of whole cloth by Jamaica's board of tourism. And while it's true that **Africans** have a sort of preternatural adoptability, it is not the case that they consume human flesh. Anymore. African blacks once believed that their gods demanded it of them to eat anyone in a pith helmet, but they now realize that those gods must be crazy.*

*In Europe, **Black Englishmen** are considered especially intelligent, for some reason, but their most visible trait is that they are probably the most fuckable people on the entire planet. In fact, the most common cause of death among blacks in England is dehydration, for exactly this reason.*

*Even within a race, physical appearances can differ slightly among populations, and **Black Swedes** are actually quite pale in color. These famous chefs and bikini team members are known for their light, blond hair, which complements their icy blue eyes.*

*Not to mention the freakish **Black Irish.***

8. At least, they all look the same to me.

One stereotype that is, unfortunately, all too true, is that blacks have shorter lifespans than other races. And it's not just because of their Herculean intake of fried chicken, crack cocaine, and menthol cigarettes. No, whether it's a war, a routine police mission, a haunted house, or an experiment involving mutated, super-intelligent sharks, blacks are the first to die in any situation. They will always be the one to receive the first stray bullet or zombie bite, and they will always be the first one sawed in half by an apron-clad maniac. It's a shame, but it's a fact of life.

While many stereotypes about blacks are harmless, a persistent and ugly rumor claims that blacks have all had their lower ribs removed in order to be able to better fellate themselves. Like all stereotypes, it is based in fact, but its prevalence is wildly exaggerated. According to my research, there is only one known case of this actually happening, when jazz legend Charlie Parker had the surgery so that he could snort heroin off of his own erect penis.

Speaking of black penises, they're huuuuuge. At least, that is the stereotype, but the myth of the huge black penis is somewhat over-blown. I've seen my share of black penises, believe you me. Dozens and dozens of them. Hundreds, even.[9] And they're nothing to sniff at: long, girthy, and they feel good in the hand. Neverthe-

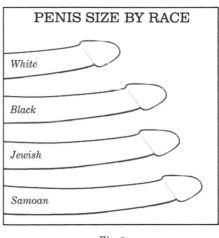

Fig. 8

9. As part of my extensive anthropological fieldwork, of course.

less, blacks don't actually have the longest penises of any race. They are outstripped by both the Samoans and the treacherous Jews. Such are the wages of sin, I suppose.

Just as black men are known, rightly or wrongly, for their large penises, black women are known for their enormous vaginas. While he was dating Whoopi Goldberg, Ted Danson famously compared sleeping with her to "throwing a hotdog down a hallway." Because Goldberg, like all black women, has a huge, cavernous vagina.

Whoopi is one example of what is known as the **Sassy Black Woman**. Perhaps the most common type of black woman, she lives in a constant state of confrontation, responding to any and all stimuli with a flamboyant finger-snapping ritual. Sassy black women are, for the most part, harmless, but in groups they can completely ruin a movie.

Fig. 9. Ted Danson reaches out to the black community.

According to the evidence I've collected from television commercials, the sassy black woman is also F.A.T. It's an acronym coined by sassy black woman Mo'Nique, or "More 'Nique," that stands for "fabulous and thick."

Of course, not all black women are sassy, and not all are fat. Some are only one or the other. Some of these sassy and/or fat black women are very successful **Black Lawyers** (who are married to successful, jazz-loving **Black Obstetricians**), while others are **Hos**.[10] For young

10. Or, in the case of the Rutgers women's basketball team, nappy-headed hos.

black women, the ho is mostly just an act, like the gangsta among young black men. They admire the scantily clad, sexually profligate women they see in rap videos, and attempt to dress and act just like them. Also, some black women are prostitutes.

Not much is known for sure about the black woman, but, as anyone who's ever picked up a copy of *National Geographic* knows, their most unique trait is that they are almost always topless.[11] It bears further study, but I believe that toplessness may be able to mend whatever racial divides still exist in this country. After all, if half-naked tribal women can effect the sexual awakenings of so many circa-1950s young white boys, then can true racial understanding be far behind?

Also, it is important to remember that you must never, under any circumstances, make a black woman take off her earrings.

CONCLUSION

Blacks are peaceful and easygoing for the most part, because of their lives of social and economic privilege. But one thing's for sure: They certainly are a musical people.

Oh, and they fucking hate the Jews.

Presumably out of penis envy.

11. *See also* King Solomon's Mines.

FURTHER READING

If you're interested in learning more about black people, here are some suggestions for further reading:

Griffin, John Howard. *Black Like Me*. Signet, 1961.

Talmadge, Herman E. *You and Segregation*. Vulcan Press, 1955.

Simpson, O. J. *If I Did It*. ReganBooks, 2006.

CHAPTER SIX

⌒◡⌒

ASIANS

A PRACTICAL GUIDE TO CELLISTS

D espite the best efforts of the United States Congress and the admissions boards of our top universities, Orientals are everywhere—some seventy billion in Asia alone. They come in all shapes and sizes, from sumo wrestlers to karate men, and they have found their way into all aspects of our culture, from video games to action movies.

In the United States, the Asian Invasion started less than 200 years ago. Toward the end of the 1800s, America's growing prosperity was drawing more and more immigrants from Asia, especially workers from China. Many of these Chinese men, or "Chinamen," were employed as manual laborers on the country's rapidly expanding rail lines, and were an integral part of the effort to build the first transcontinental railroad. In fact, many engineers still use the measurement

system that originated during that period, in which a mile is equivalent to roughly 1,760 dead Chinamen.[1]

Fig. 1. Leland Stanford and an associate managing affairs on the Central Pacific

But with this growing population of increasingly prosperous immigrants came new fears: that Asians were taking jobs from Americans and, apparently, killing white women. This was the so-called "yellow peril." The yellow peril was just as real to Americans at this time as the preceding "red peril," the later "brown peril," and the more recent "purple peril," the much-feared defensive line of the 1974 Minnesota Vikings.

Noted author H. P. Lovecraft was especially afraid of the growing Asian influence, and some of his lesser-known works reflect this preoccupa-

Fig. 2. Mickey Rooney on the set of Breakfast at Tiffany's

1. Here's a handy conversion chart for your next rail trip:

1 kilometer	~1,093 Dead Chinamen (dc)
1 furlong	~220 dc
1 nautical mile	~2,025 dc
1 league	~5,280 dc

tion. "Li Po: Reanimator," "The Doom That Came From Peking," and "Cthulhu and the Ching Chong Chinabots" are just a few of his more xenophobic stories. They tell of a mysterious, bucktoothed race of ancient Gods who urinate in other people's cola.

These fears had little basis in fact, but if there's one thing Americans hate, it's other people doing the degrading, labor-intensive jobs that they won't do themselves.[2]

Widespread outrage over the immigrants' creepy animation and brazen lack of epicanthic folds compelled Congress to pass the Chinese Exclusion Act of 1882, which barred all further immigration from China.[3] A mere sixty-one years later, this extreme measure was overturned by the more reasonable Magnuson Act of 1943, which allowed 105 whole Chinese people to enter the country every year.

But, just like Harvard's admissions guidelines, the Chinese Exclusion Act was unable to stem the tide. When their best efforts to keep Asians out of the country failed, the U.S. government took the next rational step and decided to lock them all up in camps. In these internment camps, the detainees, or "interns," would serve their time by making photocopies, doing some light filing, and fetching coffee from the Starbucks downstairs.

As John Lennon said, "Asians are the nigger of the world."

Relations are better now, and the Asians even have their own towns: low-income, high-density areas where white people go for massages and counterfeit purses. Chinatowns, Koreatowns, Japantowns, and Cambodiavilles exist in nearly every major city today. But don't worry, the locals are now free to come and go as they please. The only

2. This attitude, and the violence it often inspires, led in the eighteenth century to the near extermination of the entire native Oompa-Loompa population.
3. The President at the time was the portly Chester A. Arthur, who, ironically, had more chins than Chinatown.

known exception is the controversial maximum security Chinatown in Virginia Beach.[4]

One of the reasons that Asians are so tolerated these days is that white men really like to have sex with them. Heterosexual white men love fucking Asian women, homosexual white men love fucking Asian men, and Gary Glitter loves fucking Asian children.

Many Americans travel all the way to Asia just to fuck Asians. It's a process known as "sex tourism," and it makes up more than 90 percent of the annual GDP in most Asian countries. (The other 10 percent is mostly *Kumite*-related.)

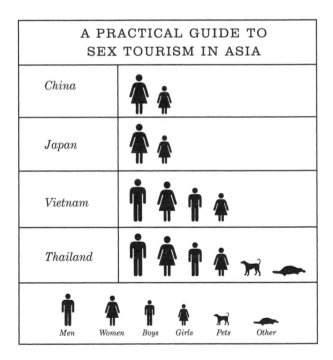

4. Despite its name, Sing Sing prison in New York is actually a mixed-race correctional facility.

Not all white men who date Asians have an Asian fetish, though. Some white men like Asians in the same way that overweight white women like black men; it's just nice to be good enough for someone. Many white men also enjoy dating small, boyish foreign women whom they can dominate, physically and emotionally, rather than face the risks of an adult relationship with a peer.

So who is the mysterious Asian? Is he megalomaniacal facial-hair enthusiast Fu Manchu? Or is he merely 1950s Atlas Comics Fu Manchu knockoff the Yellow Claw? Or even another mustachioed villain altogether?

In this country, the Asian is actually relatively harmless, and makes an excellent research assistant or adoptee. I believe that the widespread hatred and mistrust of our

Fig. 3. The mysterious Asian

mysterious neighbors to the east[5] comes more from ignorance than actual distaste. One should never underestimate the American fear of the unknown.

5. Or west, depending which way you go around.

*THINGS THAT ASIANS HAVE STOLEN
FROM THE BLACKS*

1. Kung Fu
2. Gunpowder
3. Fortune cookies
4. The blues

The root of this fear may lie in the impenetrability of the cryptic Asian language. Asian is not intuitive like our elegant, twenty-six-letter system. It is instead based on pictograms, which are small visual representations of the objects they describe.

Fig. 4. The Asian language, as featured on the classic game show Concentration

As you can see from the illustration, Asian is basically gobbledy-gook. Even worse, as a spoken language it is exclusively yelled at passersby. And these days, that communication gap isn't just unfortunate. It's downright dangerous.

Because, while the Orientals in this country are, for the most part, domesticated, there is talk of a sinister force gathering strength deep within the heart of the Asias, Major *and* Minor. It is a peril not just yellow, but red as well. The red and yellow Chinese constitute a very

real *orange menace* to our way of life, and to our women. The orange menace is churning out low-priced consumer goods at a terrifying rate, and there is nothing we can do to stop it.

TELLING THEM APART

In the face of this new orange menace, it's important to know more about the different *types* of Asians. We know how to tell them from non-Asians, but how do we tell them apart from each other?

As with most mysteries of the universe, schoolyard rhymes provide part of the answer. For example, "Chinese, Japanese, dirty knees, look at these," provides a handy guide to some of the most popular Asian races. As the rhyme explains, a Chinese person's eyes slant up at the corners, while a Japanese person's slant down. The Thai, on the other hand, are notorious for their poor hygiene, while Koreans have huge knockers.

Now let's take a look at the rest of the continent, in an exhaustively researched, country-by-country breakdown of Asiatic man.

THE PEOPLE'S REPUBLIC OF CHINA

It's hard to overestimate just how much Westerners love opium. Where would we be without it? From that first shot of black tar in the shower before work, to that last puff on the pipe at bedtime, Western society is built on its passion for disassociating itself from daily life. Whether they be religion or drugs, we just can't get enough opiates. In the eighteenth century, however, the villainous Chinese came to the ridiculous conclusion that opium is somehow harmful, and banned it.

Unwilling to do without their "Kubla Khans," their *Naked Lunches,*

and their Iggy Popses, the British continued to trade in opium illegally. When the wicked, immoral Chinese began to more rigorously enforce their ban, the British declared war and crushed the Chinese forces, first in 1840, then, again, in 1856. We sure do love opium.

A Western victory over this new orange menace will not be so easy, though. If their ability to run over college students with tanks is any indication, they are a military force to be reckoned with.

In all likelihood, no Chinese people will ever read this, because they aren't allowed to read books or look at websites not approved by the Communist regime. Which is a shame, because I think they'd really like it.

TAIWAN AND HONG KONG

Don't exist.

VIETNAM

Most people only know Vietnam as "that place what where the war was at," but it is also a ready source of attractive and affordable poontang. Unfortunately, the majority of its orifices are packed with broken glass and shrapnel.

This nation of *vagina dentatas* is still recovering from its humiliating defeat in the Vietnam War, but remains a beautifully shot journey into the horrors of man's inner struggle. Every once in a while, a lone-wolf former G.I. will travel to Vietnam to free some of the remaining American prisoners of war, of which there are many, but for the most part relations with the country are amicable. We will be forever grateful to them for lending us that kid from *Goonies* and *Temple of Doom*. He was Vietnamese, right? Cute kid.

CAMBODIA

Cambodia's tourist board is now pleased to announce six spectacular, atrocity-free getaways. Whether it's a bike ride through the beautiful killing fields, or a romantic picnic in the shadow of one of its many skull-filled *stupas*, Cambodia is a vacation destination for the entire family.

LAOS

Laotians are notoriously bad dancers. If you've ever been to a Laotian wedding you will know what I am referring to. They suffer from both a lack of rhythm and a lack of self-awareness that combine for some of the worst dancing you will ever see. Which may explain the catastrophic failure of the Southeast Asian version of *So You Think You Can Dance?*

Fig. 5. This building is full of skulls.

PACIFIC ISLANDERS

Pacific Islanders like the Hawaiians, Samoans, and Guamese are big, fat party animals. Highly recommended![6]

6. Samoans also make the most delicious of all the Girl Scout cookies.

BURMA (MYANMAR)

Burma, which is also known as Myanmar, can't seem to make up its goddamn mind about what to call itself. But it has shown its commitment to one thing: a clean-shaven face. Burma is famous for the smooth comfort of its affordable native shaving creams, and Burmese poets have long celebrated them in verse. Here is a typical example by an anonymous author:

> *A shave*
> *that's real*
> *no cuts to heal*
> *a soothing*
> *velvet after-feel*
> *Burma Shave*

Not since Irish Spring soap or French's mustard has an indigenous product been so thoroughly embraced by an entire culture.

Burma also lives under a brutal, repressive military *junta*.

THAILAND

Until 1949, Thailand was known as Siam, so called because it was the birthplace of the first Siamese twins, Chang and Eng Bunker. It was renamed, however, to cash in on the growing international popularity of Thai food,[7] and it has remained Thai-Land ever since, except for a brief period in the 1980s when it was known as "Astronaut Ice Cream-istan."

Fig. 6. Deborah Kerr,
the original sex tourist

7. Before then, thin, potent skewers of marijuana buds were known as "Siamese sticks."

SINGAPORE

Singapore is a nation of people who love whipping the bare bottoms of American teenagers with sticks. It's probably best to avoid it altogether, unless you're into that sort of thing.

KOREA

Koreans are a little tough to read. One Korean may be a helpful, eager trading partner, courteously taking in your dry cleaning or hosting the 1988 Summer Olympic Games, while another dresses in olive drab and threatens to bomb you out of existence. It's almost as if there are two different Koreas altogether.

The 38th Parallel

Fig. 7. The Korean brain

The scientific explanation for this lies in the Korean brain, which is divided into two sections. That division is known as the *38th Parallel*, and it separates the top and bottom of the brain like a sideways *corpus callosum*. Koreans who are "south-brained" tend to be calmer and more reasonable, while those who use only the top half of the brain tend to be totally batshit insane and wear enormous sunglasses.

MACAU

Due to their small size, bright plumage, and hollow bones, residents of Macau make popular pets here in America.

MALAYSIA

Malaysia is a nation of expert seamstresses and seamsters. Their skill with sewing machines and shoe leather is almost innate, which is lucky, because most of them begin work in their local factories immediately after weaning. Not surprisingly, one of the most famous Malaysians is Jimmy Choo, the shoe designer.

MALDIVES

Frankly, this series of geographically flat atolls isn't really worth talking about, because, at only two meters above sea level, it probably won't be around much longer. Sorry, Maldives. Maybe if the Jews hadn't caused global warming, you wouldn't be so royally screwed.

NEPAL, TIBET, AND BHUTAN

These mountainous countries are inhabited by a few elderly, bearded gurus, who live alone atop their various peaks. Much like the leprechauns of Ireland, finding and catching one entitles you to a share of its treasure. Unfortunately, since they do not have any worldly possessions, that treasure is mostly limited to thought-provoking but ultimately meaningless aphorisms.

Every once in a while, one of these gurus will deign to extort money from an American tourist, but most of the time they just stick to sitting cross-legged and whistling tunelessly. They should not be confused with gurus from India, who cater exclusively to British pop bands.

BRUNEI

Brunei is located on the island of Borneo, which it shares with Malaysia and Indonesia. In a very literal sense, these people from Borneo are savage, cannibalistic wildmen. They are not allowed within the borders of the United States for safety reasons, but it is rumored that their descendants have settled in the wilderness of eastern Canada.

TUVA REPUBLIC

Tuva is a mountainous region of Russia that is known for its incredibly creepy music. Tuvan monks have mastered the art of "throat singing," a technique that uses the vocal chords to sing multiple pitches at the same time. Throat singers are generally celibate, peaceful ascetics who sing for spiritual reasons, but if you can find one who does oral? Man, are you in for a treat.

MONGOLIA

Mongolia is an unfortunate case of inbreeding gone overboard. People from Mongolia ("Mongoloids") possess an extra twenty-first chromosome, which causes significant impairment in both learning and physical development. Mongoloids have a pronounced, simian brow, and often wear goony, chili bowl–style haircuts.

Most Mongoloids can be taught to read, write, and perform simple arithmetic, but their inability to progress beyond this point has crippled Mongolia's economy. While imports of toys and helmets continue to skyrocket, Mongolia's exports are limited to hand-sewn leather wallets and macaroni necklaces. However, Mongoloids are to be neither pitied nor coddled, but treated as human beings who just happen to have special needs.

INDONESIA

Indonesia is totally fucked. It has to deal with near-constant tsunamis, earthquakes, and volcano eruptions, and, every month or two, it rains frogs from the sky. Apparently, someone up there hates the Indonesians. Probably because they're Godless brown Asians.

JAPAN

Japan is a beautiful, seismically unstable archipelago of faceless businessmen and infantilized prostitutes. With a dazzling array of anime, comic books, and toys, all featuring young, busty girls in schoolgirl outfits, Japanese culture has long appealed to nerds and horny nerds alike.

And the Japanese, typified by a businessman who likes to sleep in a drawer, are horny as well. Occasionally that horniness translates into the murder of a prostitute, followed by its institutional cover-up, but there is an elaborate, Sean Connery–based system in place to handle such situations, when they occur.

Of course, not all Nipponese horniness turns deadly. Many businessmen are horny in the privacy of their own homes or sleep-drawers. In fact, the Japanese economy is largely based on the trade in soiled panties, which is its chief economic indicator.

This should help to explain some of their native customs, as well. For example, Japanese people do not bow in greeting out of politeness. Rather, they do it because they are eager to lean in and smell the crotch of everyone they meet. If someone bows to

Nikkei
Soiled Panties 225

Fig. 8. The Japanese stock market

you, you should punch them in the top of the head, because that's disgusting.

THE REST OF ASIA

Is all basically the same. An Asian can be your greatest ally or your fiercest rival; it all depends on you. In the wild, Asians live in packs, so it's important to establish yourself as the pack leader early on in the relationship. Otherwise they will never be the calm, submissive Asians that you want them to be.

While India, Bangladesh, Sri Lanka, and Pakistan are all technically part of Asia, their differentness warrants its own chapter. For more on these wily, barefoot subcontinentals, see the chapter on **Indians (and Injuns)**. As for those other countries that are technically in Asia? Russia and the 'stans? They're not really Asian. That whole area is more like a bargain basement version of Eastern Europe. So . . . not really worth discussing.

CONCLUSION

In conclusion, the Orange Menace is real and inevitable. While the ordinary Asian is relatively harmless, like ants they are a terrifying, unstoppable threat when amassed as one. Also, like ants, they are nuts for nougat.

FURTHER READING

If you're interested in learning more about the Asian peoples, here are some suggestions for further reading:

Stoddard, Lothrop. *The Rising Tide of Color Against White World-Supremacy*. Charles Scribner's Sons, 1920. (esp. "The Yellow Man Is Inferior in Every Way and Other Things I Learned At Harvard.")

Hearst, William Randolph. "Why I Hate The Filthy China-Jew," in *Collected Editorials*. Parke-Bennet Galleries, Ltd., 1938.

Lovecraft, H. P. *Cthulhu and the Ching Chong Chinabots*. Arkham House, 1939.

"Asian Hunks," *www.asianhunks.net*, 2006.

~⌒◦⌒~

MERPEOPLE

A PRACTICAL GUIDE TO OUR NEIGHBORS BENEATH THE SEA

N ot much is known about Merpeople. Few other humans have ever interacted with them, and fewer still have visited Atlantis, the city where they live beneath the sea, which is why there are so many rumors and misconceptions about them. Hopefully, this chapter will help to separate fact from fiction, and provide some insight into this misunderstood race.[1]

There are several competing theories of the origin of Merpeople. Some believe that they are a long-lost tribe from the Bible, and that

1. How do I know so much about Merpeople, you ask? Field research. The same way that great ethnographer, Samuel Taylor Coleridge, found the ancient Asian city of Xanadu, I was able to "chase the dragon" all the way to the bottom of the ocean. Of course, opium is not yet widely accepted as a historiographic method, but it provides an unbeatable first-hand experience.

Atlantis was once a terrestrial city in the Middle East. In a flood or an earthquake, this theory goes, the entire city sank, and the Merpeople who lived there were forced to evolve. Just as Jews evolved large, hooked noses to sniff out modern paper money, Merpeople developed their unique aquatic features in order to adapt to this new habitat.

Others argue that the rest of the races banded together and sank Atlantis, because of the freakish fish-people who lived there.

Either way, Merpeople—Mermen and Mermaids—now live in a small, self-segregated community on the floor of the ocean,[2] and only interact with the other races when they are drawing them to their death along the rocky shoals of the Mediterranean.

On occasion, Merpeople have been able to come on land undetected, with the help of evil, cephalopodal sea witches, but it never ends well.

Fig. 1. Mermaid

PHYSIOLOGY

Merpeople are the most distinct of all the races because of their unique physiology. There has, however, been some dispute over what exactly makes someone a Merperson. Some researchers have tried to lump in any kind of aquatic humanoid, but there are many freakish, genetic mistakes trolling the oceans, and not all of them are Merpeople.

Sea Hags, for example, have some human features, but they are

2. It is their black fraternity.

really just fish with human legs and genitalia. Sea Centaurs, Jewfish, the Welsh, and Platypuses, are, similarly, human-*like*, but not actually human.[3] Merpeople, by contrast, are a race of humans who just happen to have fish tails and gills.

One question that has sparked great debate among lonely nerds everywhere is how Merpeople reproduce. The answer is simple enough, now that we understand their biology. The male of the species, the Merman, ejaculates a cloud of spermatozoa into the water in the general area of the female Mermaid. The Mermaid accepts the seed into her semipermeable birth sac, where it fertilizes her eggs. When they are ready, she lays the eggs in a muddy riverbed, or some other suitably shallow water.

The eggs then grow into mertadpoles, and those that are not eaten by predatory fish, amphibians, and shore birds become Merpeople. It's the same way Gypsies mate, only more dignified.

Fig. 2. Not a Merman

Fig. 3. Mermen originally evolved from mermonkeys.

Fig. 4. Much of what we know about Merpeople comes from those who have been captured and vivisected.

3. Aquaman, on the other hand, turns out to be just a white guy with gills.

DISCRIMINATION

The other races have always discriminated against Merpeople, because they are so different. This may even be what drove them underwater. But I am inclined to believe that the prejudice against Merpeople comes more from ignorance than from actual dislike.

It is like our relationship with another aquatic monster, the giant squid. We are threatened by the myth of the giant squid as a fierce, many-tentacled rapist, but we can't trust everything we see in Japanese animation. Those wild tales, like the ones about Merpeople, are products of our innate human fear of the unknown.

It is also frustrating, for whites especially, not to be able to find and lynch Merpeople for their imagined crimes. The perceived cowardice in their aquatic self-segregation is why Merpeople are called the "chicken of the sea." Which is also the name of the top-selling brand of canned Mermaid-meat.

Merpeople are not without their admirers, though. Any group of outsiders, even one as universally reviled as they are, can always count on three types of people for support and adulation. Just like Christina Aguilera, *Sailor Moon*, and Gustav Klimt, Merpeople—Mermaids in particular—are idolized by little girls, horny nerds, and the gays.

Fig. 5. "A Mermaid," by John William Waterhouse, 1905. In the private collection of Andrew Lloyd Webber, and on the dorm room walls of arty girls everywhere.

Unfortunately, this niche support does little to help Merpeople with the broader population and, like Hollywood's support for Democrats, may actually hurt their cause.

COMMON STEREOTYPES

Many stereotypes exist about Merpeople, but few of them have any basis in fact. For example, there is no reason to think that Merpeople are all fish-fucking degenerates. The fish-fucking stereotype is a cruel misrepresentation of the Merperson lifestyle. Some Merpeople do have unusual tastes, it's true, but plenty of white people have sex with farm animals, and that doesn't make them all zoophiles.

Fig. 6. The heraldic shield of the Merbear community

Another myth about Mermaids is that they all wear clamshells all the time. Clamshell bikinis are occasionally worn in fashion shoots, but they are simply not practical for everyday use. They chafe the nipples, and the lack of elasticity makes them extremely difficult to keep in place. Most Mermaids actually go topless, but those who don't tend to wear sports bras.

That said, there is at least one stereotype with some truth to it: Merpeople have terrible taste. They buy more Anne Geddes photographs per capita than any other race, and their apartments look like the set of a David Lynch movie— all lacquered black particleboard and red velvet curtains. They also wear backpacks instead of shoulder bags, which makes them look like they're on their way to social studies class.

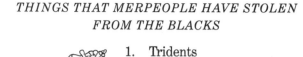

THINGS THAT MERPEOPLE HAVE STOLEN FROM THE BLACKS

1. Tridents
2. Conch shells
3. Sunken treasure
4. Aqua Boogie

CONCLUSION

These inaccurate, frequently contradictory stereotypes come from a lack of familiarity with the Merpeople. I hope that this chapter has given the reader some insight into their physiology, their culture, and their reproductive rituals, and perhaps this newfound understanding will help lead to a greater understanding among the races.

After all, we're not really so different. From the waist up, Mermen can easily be mistaken for whites, just like Centaurs, Satyrs, and the Jews.

Then again, the rest of the races aren't really filthy, fish-fucking freaks.[4]

4. Mud sharks don't count.

FURTHER READING

If you're interested in learning more about Merpeople, here are some suggestions for further reading:

Andersen, Hans Christian. *The Little Mermaid.* Golden Press, 1966.

Anderson, Elizabeth, and Temple Matthews. *The Little Mermaid II: Return to the Sea.* Disney, 2000.

Don, Ian. *Splash!* (novelization). Star Books, 1984.

CHAPTER EIGHT

ARABS

A PRACTICAL GUIDE TO A
PEACE-LOVING RACE

L et me first just say that I have nothing but respect for Arabs, and all those who practice the Arab faith.

The Arab (pronounced /'eiræb/) is a controversial figure in the modern world. Arabs have a proud history of cultural and intellectual achievement, but in recent years they have become associated with violence and intolerance.

Every day, we hear about terrorist bombings perpetrated by Arabs, and it gives some people the impression that all Arabs are dangerous *jihadists*. Attacks like the 1995 bombing of the Federal Building in Oklahoma City, by Arab militiaman Timothy McVeigh, make it hard to separate a lone nut from the race he belongs to. Not to mention the terrifying string of mail-bombings by al-Qaeda terrorist Theodore Kaczynski in the 1980s and 1990s.

Just as all squares are rectangles, but not all rectangles are squares, all terrorist attacks are carried out by Arabs, but that does not mean that every Arab is a terrorist. In fact, no more than 60 percent of living Arabs are on the U.S. government's terrorist watch list.

It's important not to make a big issue of this supposed terrorist bent. Because it's culturally insensitive, of course, but also because Arabs are the world's touchiest race.

TOUCHINESS BY RACE

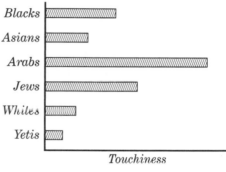

Touchiness

Fig. 1

They are extremely sensitive, and liable to be set off by even the smallest disagreement. A single unkind word, or even the appearance of one, has been known to send Arabs into an uncontrollable rage. While they are not intentionally violent, a sort of temporary insanity overtakes them when exposed to the slightest stress or confrontation, and they take to the streets by the thousands, shouting and lighting flags on fire.

Arabs all over the world rioted in 2006 when a defamatory cartoon about former U.S. President Rutherford B. Hayes was published in a Danish newspaper. In the Arab world, Rutherford B. Hayes is the most revered of all U.S. presidents, and this perceived slander against him caused an outburst of chanting, flag burning, and destruction of public property.

And that is just one example of the Arabs' notorious touchiness.

They have also rioted over offen-
sive paintings, offensive magazine
articles, and, in one case, offensive
pencil-toppers.

If it were merely a question
of civil unrest, this touchiness
might not be such a big deal, but
peoples' lives are at stake. It is a
little known fact that Arabs are
made of a highly volatile organic
compound similar to nitroglyc-
erin. Under stressful conditions,
they are liable to spontaneously
combust, and their nervous con-
stitutions cause them to do so
frequently. Often in public places,
like cafés and Israeli buses.

Fig. 2. The offending cartoon

DISCRIMINATION

It all began in the eleventh century, when whites from Europe orga-
nized an extensive military campaign against the Arabs in the Mid-
dle East. The Pope, who was then only 700 years old,[1] sent soldiers,
and even children, to harass the Arabs and drive them out of the
Holy Land.

As John Lennon said, "Arabs are the nigger of the world."

In the Pope's defense, what were Arabs doing in Jerusalem in the first

1. He is now more than 1,600, though he changes his last name every thirty years or so.

Fig. 3. An interloper in the Christian Holy Land

place? It's the most holy city in Christianity, so there's no reason it should be important to the members of any other race or religion.

After only a couple hundred years, the Crusades were declared a success, but that wasn't the end of it for the Arabs. In 1948, the United Nations stole a small strip of their land along the Mediterranean Sea, and gave it away—to the Jews, of all people.

Needless to say, the Arabs were upset. They viewed this Hebraic incursion as a direct provocation, and it led the already unstable Arab biological makeup to become increasingly volatile. It's especially galling, because the Jews now get to live peaceful, idyllic lives in Israel, while Arabs are blowing up at an alarming rate.

Since then, things have only gotten worse. The frequent explosions, coupled with the terrorist acts of a few extremists, have raised anti-

Fig. 4. Racist

Arab sentiment to new heights all around the world. Every day, Arabs must face discrimination, stereotyping, and even violence, both in the Middle East and abroad. In America, blue-collar comedians, country singers, and producer Joel Surnow are some of the most brutal persecutors of the Arab race. The recording artist Toby Keith personally beats the living crap out of anyone wearing a turban.[2]

2. Keith is widely credited with the 2004 rape and murder of Palestinian leader Yasser Arafat.

It's gotten to the point where no Arab is safe. In order to keep them out of harm's way, the U.S. government has been moving as many Arabs as possible into indefinite protective custody on a military base in Cuba.

PROMINENT ARABS

Much of the discrimination Arabs face comes from the ignorant belief that they are a violent, warlike people. Non-Arabs see villains like Ayatollah Khomeini and the supporting cast of 24, and they assume that all Arabs are involved in a holy war against "The Great Satan."[3] Nothing could be further from the truth, and the following are just a few of the many prominent, successful Arabs who prove the lie to this hateful misconception.

- Sheik Yerbouti — *The esteemed Sheik is a member of the Arab royal family, as well as a Grammy nominee.*
- The Iron Sheik — *This fearsome wrestler defeated Bob Backlund for the World Wrestling Federation heavyweight title in 1983, only to lose it to Hulk Hogan four weeks later.*
- Tony Shalhoub — *A former cab driver, Shalhoub is now a successful private detective.*
- Mahmoud Abdul-Rauf — *This former NBA Most Improved Player spent most of his career with the Den-*

3. "The Great Satan" is actually not America's worst nickname. That honor goes to "Fuckface McFiftystates."

ver *Nuggets, as well as a few years with the Sacramento Kings and Vancouver Grizzlies.*

- Ishtar — *Even though it has become a laughingstock,* Ishtar *is actually very entertaining.*
- Osama bin Laden — *A substantial family inheritance allowed bin Laden the freedom to develop his skills as a theologian and an orator, and he has become one of the foremost religious leaders in the entire Arab world.*
- Jesus — *Everyone always accuses the Arabs of killing Jesus, but not many people know that he was actually an Arab himself. It is easy to forget that the Christian messiah was born in the Middle East and raised in Egypt.*

COMMON STEREOTYPES

Unfortunately, the hundreds of peaceful, friendly Arabs out there have done little to dissuade the rest of the world from their prejudices. That is why we still have stereotypes like the **Faceless, Screaming Mob.** It is true that many Arabs assemble into faceless, screaming mobs when they are offended, or cranky, or bored, but this is hardly a uniquely Arab trait. It is also common in Hispanics, students, and the French.

The stereotype of the **Genie** is equally unjustified. No one will deny that some Arabs have blue skin and take fey, baggy-pantsed young men as their traveling companions, but the vast majority do not. Even

those who are manic, family-friendly comic impressionists rarely have the power to grant wishes or shapeshift.

Arab women are more easily typed, and the most common is the **Odalisque**. Sensuous and decadent, the odalisque whiles away the hours smoking *kif* on silk pillows in the company of muscular eunuchs. Her days are occasionally broken up only by giving birth to a child of the man who owns her.

This man is often a **Sheik**. In his flowing robes, this bearded *emir* spends most of his time managing his harems, bathing in pools of crude oil and caviar, and building enormous theme hotels.

At the opposite end of the social scale is **Ali Baba**, the camel-riding thief who lives in a magical cave with forty other men. Not that there's anything wrong with that.

THINGS ARABS HAVE STOLEN
FROM THE BLACKS

1. Cassius Clay
2. Lew Alcindor
3. Wesley Cook
4. The prison population

THE ARAB WORLD

There are also more subtle cultural differences among the different populations of Arabs. Let us now look at the Arab race, country by country.

OMAN

The Omani, like many Arabs, are incredibly horny. They have to cover their women from head to toe in thick cloth, because even the slightest glimpse of a bare female ankle sends them into a sexually violent frenzy. If Arab women had any rights or legal status, the Omani Special Victims Unit would be positively overwhelmed.

UNITED ARAB EMIRATES

The UAE is home to Dubai, the world's most hedonistic, amoral city. If you've ever wanted to snowboard down an indoor ski slope while target-shooting endangered Bengal tigers, this is the place to go. The rest of the Arab world is morally opposed to eating pork, but in Dubai there's actually an entire luxury hotel constructed of nothing but.

LIBYA

Libya is perhaps most famous for the shores of Tripoli, where, after kicking some Hispanic ass in the halls of Montezuma, U.S. Marines came to bust some heads in the First Barbary War.

YEMEN

The Yemeni are a pair of twins who have been immortalized in both Greek mythology and crackpot astrology. Some Yemeni have the power to take the forms of different animals or, less impressively, of water, but they must first join hands in order to do so.

LEBANON

Lebanon is the rest of the Middle East's bitch. Its citizens are noteworthy, however, for their powerful and accurate throwing arms.

IRAQ

Iraqis are an extremely ungrateful people, and frequently live in rubble-strewn areas without any sort of infrastructure whatsoever. If they had a better attitude, they might not live in such wretched conditions.

AFGHANISTAN

Afghanis are an extremely ungrateful people, and frequently live in rubble-strewn areas without any sort of infrastructure whatsoever. Their shawls, however, are exquisite.

IRAN

The Iranians just want to be the center of attention. If you ignore them, they'll go away. Either that, or bomb us out of existence. One or the other.

SAUDI ARABIA

Other oil-rich countries could learn from the Saudis. They subjugate women and quash free speech without making a big thing about it, and have the good sense to maintain strong diplomatic ties to the United States.

EGYPT

Egypt is the birthplace of Charlton Heston, one of America's most revered elder statesmen. When he was born, he was placed in a basket and set among the reeds, only to be discovered by the pharaoh's daughter, who raised him as a prince. When he was old enough to discover who he really was, he took up arms against the fascist anti-gun movement and led his people to freedom.

JORDAN

Jordan—last name Ladd—is the daughter of former *Charlie's Angels* star Cheryl Ladd and the granddaughter of actor Alan Ladd. Despite having a breast reduction at age sixteen, Ladd has become an established actress on the indie film circuit.

TWO KINDS OF ARABS

In a broader sense, there are two main types of Arabs: *Sunnis* and *Shias*, and the differences between the two groups are utterly irreconcilable. If you've ever read about violence or conflict among the Arabs, this is the root of it. The intra-Arab discrimination that occurs between them is, in many ways, more damaging than any slurs or preemptive wars ever could be.

Some people are confused by the doctrinal and ideological rift between Sunnis and Shias, but it's actually quite simple. The conflict goes all the way back to the chaotic period following the death of the prophet Mohammed, when the leadership of the Arab race was in flux. Shias believe that the succession passed to Ali, Mohammed's son-in-law and the father of his grandchildren by Fatima. Sunnis, on the other hand, believe that the succession passed to Umar, who was elected by the Arab people in a democratic *shura*. Shias now follow only divinely appointed, infallible descendants of the prophet Mohammed, while Sunni *caliphs* are elected by shura.

Shias also have an entire additional sentence in their *adhan*, the call to prayer. And, when they go to *salah*, Shias pray to their god, whom Arabs call *Allah*, by placing their foreheads on the ground or on a clay surface, rather than on a prayer mat like Sunnis. And that

doesn't even begin to scratch the surface of their contrary positions on *mutah*.

So it's obvious why they would want to kill each other.

Of course, one thing does bring Sunnis and Shias together: a violent, abiding hatred of the Jews.

Fig. 5. See?

CONCLUSION

The Arabs are responsible for much of what we think of as modern civilization, from government and architecture, to geometry, naval exploration, and *shawarma*.[4] Unfortunately, the race's most public figures are a marginalized extremist movement that is doing its best to blow all of that up.

4. Not to mention the mythical *shawarma-lafel*.

The key to combating extremist groups like al-Qaeda and the Taliban is to do everything we can to make *all* Arabs hate America. That way, those extremists groups won't actually be so extreme, and we can fight a race war, rather than an ideological one.

So far, U.S. foreign policy is doing an extraordinary job of making that dream a reality.

FURTHER READING

If you're interested in learning more about the Arab people, here are some suggestions for further reading:

Rumsfeld, Donald, Paul Wolfowitz, et al. *Rebuilding America's Defenses*. Project for the New American Century, 2000.

$\sim\!\!\sim\!\!\circ\!\!\subset\!\!\sim$

GYPSIES

A PRACTICAL GUIDE TO CARNIES

G ypsies are perhaps the most hated of all the races. The ethnicities of the world are divided by all manner of strife and conflict, but the one thing that they all have in common is an abiding disdain for the Gypsy race.

Do the *Roma* people deserve it? The short answer is "yes."

The longer answer is also "yes," with an explanation. The best scientific knowledge suggests that Gypsies are genetically predisposed to thievery, prevarication, and poor personal hygiene. Not every Gypsy is a thief, a liar, or unwashed, but the vast majority of them are, in fact, all three.

As John Lennon said, "Gypsies are the nigger of the world."

The Gypsies' ancestral home is Eastern Europe, but they are, by

nature, wanderers, because they are driven away from anywhere they try to settle. Their travels take them all over the globe, from carnivals in Scandinavia, to tent shows in Australia, to state fairs here in the United States, and their caravans can be found circled on the outskirts of towns and cities in every part of the world. From these ragged encampments, the Roma run illicit gambling and prostitution rings, and mix their potions and spells in large iron cauldrons. Like parasites, they take on the characteristics of their hosts, so there is

Fig. 1. Gypsy. Tramp. Thief.

no single Gypsy archetype, but there are some traits common to the population as a whole.

Despite, or perhaps because of this wandering outcast existence, Gypsies have captured the imagination of our popular culture. Hundreds of songs have been written about Gypsies, from Santana's "Black Magic Woman" to 1934's "Race of Thieves," performed by Billy McCready's Popular Song-time Orchestra.

A romantic image is often painted of the Gypsies as carefree travelers, traipsing the world in search of love and adventure. In fact, this is directly at odds with the reality of their existence. Their out-

Fig. 2. A Gypsy encampment

fits are cobbled together from fabric and hoop earrings discarded by others, and they live on a diet of homemade suet and pruno. They have the power to see the future, and to place curses on their enemies, but this has not brought them prosperity. Their Gypsy powers have only led to more hardship, which is why they are compelled to steal.

Let us now look at the rich cultural history of these nomadic ragamuffins.

COMMON GRIFTS

THE PICKPOCKET

This simplest and most common Gypsy scam has existed for thousands of years, and takes many forms. Most often, a dexterous thief simply reaches into the mark's pocket, purse, or bag and removes his wallet. Some Gypsies will use a knife or razor to actually slice open the pocket instead of reaching into it, or cut the strap of a purse in order to remove it entirely. Gypsies may be the world's most gifted pickpockets, though British street urchins can also be surprisingly adept.

THE BABY TOSS

The *Baby Toss* is a form of pickpocketing that requires at least two Gypsies to pull off. The first throws a baby—often stolen—at the mark, and when he drops his bags to catch the airborne infant, the other Gypsy swoops in and steals his luggage.

THE SAVAGE BEATING

Another variation on the classic *Pickpocket*, this old Gypsy confidence trick finds the mark set upon by one or more thieves. After they beat him to within an inch of his life or beyond, they relieve him of his wallet and run off. Even the threat of a savage beating can be enough to trick someone into handing over their possessions, though. It must be embarrassing to fall for this old scam.

THE ORGAN DONOR

Of course, Gypsies don't just target your material possessions. Some also have their eyes on your internal organs, which can fetch a healthy sum on the black market. Stealing organs was originally an Asian scam, but the Gypsies have adopted it as well. It usually begins with the mark being seduced by a beautiful Gypsy woman, who then drugs him and leaves him for dead. When the victim awakes, he finds himself in a bathtub full of ice, with one or both kidneys missing. This scam may also overlap with the *Savage Beating*.

THE SPANISH PRISONER

This grift involves forcing the mark to watch Rebecca Pidgeon read her husband's stilted, staccato dialogue for ninety excruciating minutes.

THE GORILLA-GRAM

The classic *Gorilla-Gram* scam has been around for as long as time itself, or at least since the advent of the legitimate gorilla-gram. A trained gorilla comes to the victim's front door, claiming to have a gorilla-borne telegram from a friend or loved one. When the mark opens the door, the gorilla knocks him unconscious and a small band of Gypsy handlers cleans out his home.

THE TOOTHBRUSH IN THE RECTUM

A Gypsy with access to the mark's toiletries, most often a chamber-maid, inserts his toothbrush into her rectum, while a confederate photographs the incident. Later, they mail him the photographs, showing that the toothbrush the mark has been putting in his mouth was once in the rectum of a Gypsy scam artist. Money is rarely exchanged.

THE STEVIE NICKS

The *Stevie Nicks* is a variation on the old *Fleetwood Mac*, except that it can be performed solo. The Gypsy emits an unbearable screeching sound, which incapacitates the victim. While he is rolling on the floor, clutching his ears in pain, his wallet is stolen.

Fig. 3. Nicks and an unknown male associate

THE LITTLE MAN

This scam involves a comically small Gypsy or Wayans brother, who pretends to be an abandoned baby. When he is adopted by an idealistic young couple, the tiny Gypsy insinuates himself into their household and then robs them blind. The scam has been known to go wrong when the pint-sized criminal becomes emotionally attached to his victims, and in the end learns a valuable lesson about love and family.

THE BADGER GAME

The *Badger Game* is an attempt to extort money from married or respectable men. The mark is seduced or coerced into an extramarital affair, or the appearance thereof, with a beautiful Gypsy woman

or woodland creature. He is then threatened with exposure if he does not pay an exorbitant amount of money. Married or not, it is always important to find a secure location before sleeping with a mysterious Gypsy woman, or entering into any kind of physical relationship with a badger, raccoon, or ferret.

THE FORTUNE-TELLER

One of the few legitimate career options available to Gypsies is prognostication, which makes this scam all the more insidious. The mark is lured into the den of a supposed fortune-teller, and then given incorrect information about his future in exchange for money. It is hard to prosecute, because the full extent of the scam may not be revealed until months or even years after the encounter.

THE FOREIGN BRIDE

In this scam, the mark enters into a long-distance flirtation with a beautiful Gypsy woman he has never met. The victim falls in love with his distant paramour, and the Gypsy agrees to be married, but claims that she cannot afford to make the trip. After the victim sends the money to pay for her voyage, she requests additional funds. When he is no longer willing or able to send more money, the Gypsy disappears. Society as a whole is another victim of the *Foreign Bride*, since it lays bare the unspeakable loneliness and alienation that lies at its very heart.

THE DATE RAPE

In this old grift, a Gypsy arranges a romantic encounter with a credulous mark. Once they are on the date, the Gypsy has nonconsensual sex with the victim. Those who fall for this scam are often too embarrassed to even report it to the police.

THE CHILI BOWL

A Gypsy purporting to be a chef claims that his chili is the best in the entire world, convincing the mark to pay an inflated price in order to sample this legendary chili. When the mark receives his bowl, however, it is empty, and the Gypsy has disappeared.

THE THINNER

The *Thinner* requires the obese mark to receive oral sex from his wife while driving. When the distracted driver runs over and kills an old Gypsy woman with his car, her father places a curse on the victim causing him to lose weight until he wastes away and dies. Afterward, the Gypsy takes his wallet.

THE MARRIAGE

After a long period of courtship, a Gypsy woman uses sex, companionship, and good conversation to trick the mark into proposing to her. Over the years, the Gypsy gives birth to several of the victim's children, but the marriage seems increasingly loveless and hollow, based more on convenience and obligation than affection. Finally, the mark gives up on couples therapy and files for divorce, ceding half his assets to the Gypsy. This is known in the business as a "long con."

THE WALLET INSPECTOR

The Gypsy in this scam convinces the mark that he is a government official who enforces compliance with his country's strict wallet-safety rules. When the mark surrenders his wallet for inspection, the Gypsy absconds with it.

THE DJANGO REINHARDT

A three-fingered Gypsy, with the aid of a French violinist confederate, extorts money from music hall owners in exchange for his services as a virtuoso jazz guitarist.

Fig. 4. Gross

THE GYPSY ROSE LEE

In this elaborate "big store" scam, an overbearing Gypsy stage mother pushes her daughter into burlesque dancing. The daughter eventually becomes an international superstar, and the musical based on their relationship becomes a modern classic. The victims are the audience members for the 1998 adaptation starring Debbie Gibson,[1] who were scammed out of $100 apiece.

THE UNDERCOVER COP

A Gypsy approaches the mark and pretends to be an undercover cop. He claims that the mark is a suspect in a crime, and confiscates all of his personal possessions. Akin to the *Wallet Inspector*, except this one is easier to avoid, because while some Gypsies can find employment as low-level wallet inspectors, there are no Gypsy police officers.

THE TIP JAR

In this grift, the Gypsy visits a coffee shop. When the barista turns around to make his latte, the Gypsy reaches into her tip jar and steals the money.

1. Sorry, "Deborah" Gibson.

THE LOTTERY

The Gypsy and his confederates run a lottery game, allowing participants to buy tickets for a chance to win a large prize, often in the millions of dollars. However, the chances of winning are so infinitesimally small that the ticket is, economically speaking, worth only a fraction of the price that the mark pays for it. By selling false hope to tens of millions of the working poor, the Gypsy is effectively stealing from them.

THE DUKE LACROSSE PLAYER

In an attempt to gain personal notoriety, a Gypsy district attorney accuses three white, suburban college students of raping a black stripper. The three marks are vilified in the press, despite the existence of clear exculpatory evidence.

THE EBAY AUCTION

Fraudulent electronics, stamps, or memorabilia are put up for auction. After the mark has already paid for his purchase, he discovers that it is fake, broken, or does not exist at all, but the Gypsy seller is nowhere to be found. I'm looking at you, RomaSeller26.

PHISHING

An Internet scam in which the Gypsy sends the mark a series of unsolicited e-mails regarding insufferable jam bands. The mark then has to pay him to stop. Sometimes called *String Cheese Incidenting*.

THE ZOLTAR MACHINE

Frustrated by his small stature, a young boy asks a Gypsy machine to make him "big" in exchange for money. When the mark wakes up the

next day, he is a grown man, but this soon grows tiresome, and there is no way to change back. Needless to say, the Zoltar machine keeps the nickel.

THE RUBE GOLDBERG

This scam begins when a Gypsy leaves an urgent message for the mark. When the mark returns the call, the ringing phone at the other end startles a parrot. The parrot flaps its wings, upsetting the cup of water resting precariously on its perch. The water spills to the bottom of the cage, where it drips out onto a seesaw, the other side of which is blocking a pool ball from rolling down an incline. When the seesaw rises, the pool ball rolls and hits a bottle, spinning it around. The neck of the bottle is attached to a string, which pulls the switch on an electric fan. The electric fan blows a small toy car with a sail attached to it across a table, where it knocks over a cup of marbles. The marbles fall onto a paddle-wheel, causing it to rotate and hit a lever, which opens the door separating two sections of a hamster's cage. Starved for exercise, the hamster goes through the door into the other section, where it starts running on its wheel. The kinetic energy produced by the hamster's wheel powers a small generator, which in turn powers a machine that uses the mark's Social Security number to apply for a credit card.

THE CASTING COUCH

A Gypsy pretends to be a casting agent for a major motion picture or television show. When young actresses come in to audition, he offers them a part in a nonexistent production in exchange for having sex with him. After "sealing the deal," he promises to call with more information, but never does, since he is not a real casting agent.

THE SNAKE OIL SALESMAN

Like the *eBay Auction* scam, this grift uses misrepresented merchandise to extort money from the mark. The Gypsy offers for sale a medicinal tonic, or a healing remedy such as chiropractics, that is useless or even harmful. After the Gypsy has left town with his money, the victim discovers that this "miracle cure" is nothing more than the glandular secretions of a common garter snake.

THE SIGN OF THE GYPSY QUEEN

Popularized by Nova Scotian rock band April Wine, the *sign of the Gypsy Queen* is a scam that trades on the Gypsy reputation for black magic. A Gypsy woman warns the mark to pack his things and leave, or else face a terrible curse. Whatever the victim leaves behind is stolen.

THE PYRAMID SCHEME

In a scam that goes back thousands of years, credulous investors are compelled to build enormous sandstone tombs for the pharaohs of ancient Egypt. The Gypsy claims that the marks will realize high returns on their initial investment if they recruit others to do the same. In the end, all the money goes toward building the enormous stone edifices, and the marks are left penniless or dead from exhaustion.

Fig. 5. Suspected Gypsy Charles Ponzi

THE LOUIS VUITTON HANDBAG

Most frequently practiced by Chinese Gypsies, the *Louis Vuitton Handbag* involves selling counterfeit merchandise at prices well below those of the authentic items. The mark believes she has found a bar-

gain, only to discover afterward that her purchase is a cheap knockoff. As with many Gypsy scams, it punishes the mark for her greediness, and for being the sort of reprehensible person who actually cares what brand of handbag she owns.

THE ORGANIZED RELIGION

Preying on the hopeless and naive, the Gypsy convinces large groups of marks that there is a being with superpowers who lives in the sky, and that they should worship and fear him. The Gypsy then extorts money from the victims in the name of this "God," offering only hope and comfort in return.

Fig. 6. A real moneymaker

THE PORAJMOS

In this grift, Nazis decimate the Gypsy population of central Europe. This is actually more of a Nazi scam.

CONCLUSION

Prejudice against the Gypsies is widespread, but not undeserved. They are a lying race of thieves and tricksters with only one thing on their mind: separating you from your money. That said, racial discrimination is never acceptable, and the Roma people have endured too much of it over the years. Perhaps, using outreach and understanding rather than hate, we can learn to understand and, eventually, control these subhuman criminals. Of course, like dogs and children, some races are simply unteachable.

In the meantime, Gypsies have received reparations from some of

their worst tormentors, in the form of boxes of free, brightly colored rags. While Gypsies are not allowed to open casinos, like the Injuns, police in most countries turn a blind eye to their illegal monte operations. They are de facto allowed to operate one-, two-, three-, and even four-card monte games, and Asian monte games in a separate room.

FURTHER READING

If you're interested in learning more about the Roma people, here are some suggestions for further reading:

Laurents, Arthur. Book. Theater Communications Group, 1994.
Sondheim, Stephen. Lyrics. Theater Communications Group, 1994.
Styne, Jule. Music. Theater Communications Group, 1994.

APPENDIX ONE

SEXUAL RACES

O ur familiar, nine-race schema offers a great deal of insight into the modern world, and the human race as a species, but within each race there are also subgroups and populations that deserve their own consideration. As we have seen in previous chapters, groups like the Japanese and the Chinese can be very different from each other, even though they exist within the larger Oriental race.

By "sexual races," I don't mean the naked crabwalk that couples do every summer at Hyannis. I'm talking about ethnicities that are determined by characteristics related to sexuality, rather than country of origin or skin color. I am speaking, of course, about **Gays, Lesbians**, and **Women**.

WOMEN

It is surprising that anthropologists have not chosen to classify women as an entirely different species, since they are essentially biologically different from all other humans. They are smaller, on average, than a normal person, with wider hips and larger breasts, and their hair tends to be longer and nicer smelling.

Some women are able to pass for men, just as light-skinned blacks once tried to pass for white, but women like Brandon Teena and Hillary Clinton are the exception, not the rule.

These short, curvy creatures may sound like something out of a child's book of oddities, but they're more common than you think. And their outward appearance isn't even the strangest aspect of a woman's anatomy. *That* would be the genitalia. A woman's pudendum does not protrude at all, and is actually concave, forming a cavity within her body. It is almost the inverse of a normal human penis.

Female genitalia are, without question, gross, but they can also be dangerous. Without proper care and treatment, a woman's genitals can bleed as often as once a month, and for as long as a week at a time, which is enough to kill most people. The best way to handle this kind of bleeding is for the victim to be sequestered in a tent for the entire length of the ordeal.

Aside from their biological abnormalities, the biggest difference between women and normal humans is that women are sexually attracted to men. This highly unusual socio-sexual inclination is one of the main reasons why women are second-class citizens in our society. Even if they're doing the exact same work, someone who is attracted to men doesn't deserve to earn as much money as someone who isn't.

Like most minorities, women have their own mediocre confrontational art and literature. Most of it reeks of sour grapes, and what

doesn't come from bitterness tends to be borderline pornographic, like the paintings of Georgia O'Keeffe or the sculpture of Eva Hesse. Which is hardly surprising, coming from a race so physically and emotionally perverted. I dare anyone to look at those so-called *objets d'art* and not get an erection.[1]

That's not to say that women are necessarily "bad." They are simply "different" and "less than." There have been many great women over the years: performers like Jenna Jameson, Tera Patrick, and Linda Lovelace, politicians like Abigail Adams, Eleanor Roosevelt, and Lady Bird Johnson; and writers like Evelyn Waugh.

LESBIANS

Lesbians are an odd case. In appearance, they are like women, except without all the frilly pink outfits and tiaras, but they are less outré than women, because they are not sexually attracted to men. Lesbians have all the physical oddities of the female race, but emotionally they are just like normal human beings.

You might think that this unique orientation would pose a problem for Lesbians in their capacity as breeders, but they have figured out a way around it: borrowing sperm from David Crosby. While the genetic material is somewhat compromised by the presence of David Crosby's DNA, it is nonetheless a perfectly viable method of reproduction.

Lesbians are hindered in their everyday lives by their abnormal biology, but many have gone on to live ordinary, fulfilling lives. There are Lesbian coaches, Lesbian gym teachers, and Lesbian personal trainers, not to mention Lesbian athletes. Two Lesbians were even immortalized in the film *Monster*, by the beautiful, non-Lesbian actresses Charlize Theron and Christina Ricci.

1. Except, of course, for a woman, because she would be incapable of doing so.

Some people talk about "hot Lesbian action," as if the sexual congress of two Lesbians is somehow arousing or attractive. As someone who has met several real-life Lesbians, let me assure you that it is nothing of the kind.

GAYS

Gays are perhaps the most perplexing of all the sexual races. They have normal human bodies, but are somehow sexually attracted to men. Scientists have been unable to explain this unusual phenomenon, but they have determined that being Gay is genetic. Gay is passed down from generation to generation, father to son, even if the bloodline has been diluted by interbreeding with non-Gays. It only takes one drop of Gay blood to make you Gay, just like with blacks.

Gay people have a distinctive, sashaying walk, limp wrists, and a telltale lisp when they talk. They are also known for their love of musical theater, interior design, and fashion, but there is nothing they enjoy more than offensive, outdated stereotypes. Except, perhaps, for cock.

As any normal child learns at an early age, from movies, television, and peers, Gays are terrifying. They are waiting around every corner to corrupt our society and anally rape us. They are morally bankrupt, degenerate outsiders who are condemned by every major culture and religion. In fact, being Gay is probably the worst thing in the entire world.

Of course, being Gay isn't the same thing as engaging in homosexual behavior, which everyone does in boarding school, college, and grad school. And at parties. That is just natural experimentation, but Gay people are born Gay.

OTHERS

There are other, even smaller populations of sexual ethnicities, which we don't have space to discuss in detail here. These are races like Trannies, which can really surprise you if you don't watch out, and Bisexuals, which don't actually exist.

For a more in-depth look at these sexual ethnicities, including a rare, South African race with dogs' heads where their genitals should be, I recommend going on your computer and typing "gay sex" into your search engine.

ANCIENT RACES

Thousands of years before the modern genetic picture took shape, the world was populated by dozens of different ethnicities, many of them the ancestral forebears of the races we know today. Arabs and blacks, for example, are both descended from the ancient Ottomans, among others, while the Hispanic line can be traced all the way back to the Lusitanians and the Phoenicians.

There are nine races in the world today, but things used to be much more complicated. Limited contact among the peoples of the Earth allowed for the existence of many small, geographically distinct ethnicities that have long since died off or been assimilated. The following are just a small sample of the ancient races that once populated the earth.

PHOENICIANS

The Phoenicians were one of the first great races of sea explorers, and may be the ancestors of our modern Merpeople. For hundreds of years, they traded dyes and spices throughout the coastal regions of the Mediterranean, and, just like every other ancient race, they discovered the Americas before Columbus.

GREEKS

The ancient Greeks were divided into several different races, like the Spartans, the Thebans, and the Athenians, but the one thing they all had in common was ostentatious, unapologetic pederasty. For this reason, some have suggested that they are the ancestors of the modern Czechs, but no definitive link has been established.

ROMANS

The Romans were also known for their sexual profligacy, as documented by the great historian and filmmaker, Bob Guccione, in his *Caligula*.

CELTICS

The ancient Celtics (pronounced "sel-tiks") lived in what is now Ireland, and were known for their athletic prowess, and for inventing parquet.

VISIGOTHS

Even though the Visigoths are in all my encyclopædias and atlases, I don't think they ever actually existed. It's like when dictionary publishers put in fake words, just to find out who's copying them, only no one ever caught it.

SUMERIANS

The Sumerians were among the very first true civilizations, and their legends make up the *Epic of Gilgamesh*. These great achievements are overshadowed, however, by the fact that Sumerians were jerks. They frequently and unrepentantly showed up to parties without any alcohol of their own, slept with other peoples' girlfriends, and keyed random barrows for no reason.

EGYPTIANS

Despite being African, the Egyptians were at the forefront of cultural and technological innovation, and built the three great pyramids at Giza, using only tens of thousands of slave laborers. Historians like Erich von Däniken and the producers of *Stargate* have theorized that the Egyptians were assisted by a group of ancient alien visitors, but it is more likely that they just got the Jews to do it for them.

OTTOMANS

The Ottomans have nothing to do with what we think of as ottomans today. No, the Ottomans were entirely devoted to the design, manufacture, and sale of small decorative footstools.

VIKINGS

The Vikings were another one of the hundreds of ancient civilizations to have discovered the New World before Columbus, led there by the great sailor and warrior, Leif Garrett. Not long after, an intoxicated Garrett crashed his *knaar*, rendering his passenger, and best friend, a quadriplegic. The resulting shame spiral, and Garrett's lifelong battle with substance abuse, ultimately dissolved the Viking civilization.

SAXONS

The Saxons were a group of savages in Northern Germany. Their expanse began slowly, with the annexation of Czechoslovakia and Poland, but in the fifth century A.D. they made a swift and brutal march to the British Isles. It was during that invasion that they hooked up with the Anglos, and the pairing laid the groundwork for British culture for centuries to come, from Geoffrey Chaucer to Robbie Williams.

ELAMITES

The Elamites were the rednecks of the ancient Near East, with poor hygiene, little to no education, and cart parts strewn across their front lawns. All of which provided material for Elamite comedian Untash-Napirisha. His most famous joke, as best we can re-create it, goes like this: If you live and farm in the fertile lowlands beneath the Zagros Mountains . . . you *might* be an Elamite. It wasn't any funnier then than it is now, which is probably why he was stoned to death in 800 B.C.

GAULS

The Gauls are the ancestors of today's Frenchmen, as evidenced by their haughty, imperious manner and their total surrender to the Romans.

PERSIANS

The Persians were a race of transvestite monsters, led by a huge bald freak with swords for arms. So it's a clear line from them to the present-day Iranians.

HITTITES

The Hittites were based in Hatussas, the capital of their Near Eastern empire, and they loved pornography. They left behind thousands of clay tablets from their archives, and almost 90 percent of them were covered in cuneiform erotica. It's very hard to make two clay tablets stick together in such an arid environment, but archaeologists have found that a large portion of the tablets are, in fact, stuck together.

BABYLONIANS

According to the historian David Gray, the Babylonians were all about living in the moment. They were able to let go their hearts, let go their heads, and feel it now. Babylon, Babylon.

NUBIANS

Nubians were a forebear of modern blacks, but in them we see none of the character or social grace that characterizes black people today. Many of the confusing, hurtful stereotypes about blacks actually come from historical descriptions of the ancient Nubians; they were a lazy race of promiscuous, unintelligent criminals. The Nubians are still remembered for one major breakthrough, though: They were the first civilization to use unconventional time signatures.

SABINES

The Sabines were one of the first civilizations in ancient, tribal Italy, but they are most famous for having all of their women kidnapped and raped by the Romans. So, while the Sabines died out, their bloodline lived on through their wives' offspring. Which is probably kind of a cold comfort.

DOOZERS

The Doozers were an industrious, ant-like people, who spent their days building intricate scaffolding made of radishes. The goal of that construction work was for it to be eaten by the Fraggles, which proved not to be a sustainable existence for the Doozers.

APPENDIX THREE

INTERRACIAL DATING

Dating between the races is common, but not encouraged. If you do plan to procreate interracially, I encourage you to laminate this chart and keep it in your wallet at all times.

WHO LIKES WHO

White women	Black men
Black women	Black men
Jewish women	Jewish men
Quebecois women	Quebecois men
Asian women	Asian men
Mermaids	Mermen
Phoenician women	Phoenician men
Injun women	Injun men
Arab women	Arab men
Indian women	Indian men
Gypsy women	Gypsy men
Hispanic women	Hispanic men

White men	Asian women
Black men	Asian women
Jewish men	Asian women
Quebecois men	Asian women
Asian men	Cartoon characters
Mermen	Asian women
Phoenician men	Carthaginian women
Injun men	Asian women
Arab men	Asian women
Indian men	Asian women
Gypsy men	Anything that moves
Hispanic men	American jobs

QUESTIONABLE RACES

If the following groups do, in fact, qualify as human, then they are unique ethnicities, but further study is required before we can make any final judgments.

Maori	Femmes	Gelflings
Socialites	Radishes	Belgians
Sandwich Islanders	Muppets™	Coppolas
Yetis	Newfies	Australopithecines
Sasquatches	Laplanders	Germans
Bigfoots	Tribbles	Expressionists
Abominable Snowmen	Triffids	Cablinasians
	Bratz	Azaleas
Quebecois	Poor People	Strippers
Thundercats	Goombas	Catholics
Batboys	Koopa Troopas	Battletoads
The Elderly	Draculas	Yalies
Puggles	Baristas	Elephant Men

THE GOOD ONES

PROMINENT, HARMLESS MEMBERS
OF EACH RACE

WHITES

 Dan Whitney

 Ron White

 Jeff Foxworthy

 Bill Engvall

BLACKS

 Colin Powell

 Alfonse Ribeiro

 Kevin Federline

HISPANICS

 J-Lo

 Shakira

 Charo

JEWS

> George Allen
>
> Jesus

INJUNS

> The Atlanta Brave
>
> The Cleveland Indian
>
> The Washington Redskin
>
> The Kansas City Chief
>
> The Florida State Seminole

ASIANS

> Ryu
>
> Link
>
> Starfox
>
> Kid Icarus

GYPSIES

> Stevie Nicks
>
> Cher

ARABS

> King Abdullah bin Abdul Aziz al Saud of Saudi Arabia (for now)
>
> Sultan Qaboos bin Said al Said of Oman (for now)
>
> President Khalifa bin Zayed Al Nahyan of the United Arab Emirates (for now)
>
> President Ali Abdullah Saleh of Yemen (for now)

GAYS

Ken Mehlman
Mark Foley
Larry Craig
Ted Haggard
Bill Frist

WOMEN

Dame Edna
RuPaul
Tootsie

MERPEOPLE

Prince Atlantius
Neptunia
Maria Shriver

QUEBECOIS

None

CRANIA OF THE RACES
INCLUDING THAT OF FREDERICK SCHILLER

(From Nott, Josiah Clark. *Indigenous Races of the Earth*. J.B. Lippincott & Co., Philadelphia, 1857.)

BUSHMAN

SCLAVONIAN

KALLIN

ASHANTEE

TURK

ASSYRIAN

SAMOLENE

HINDOO

MUMMIED
NEGRESS

ABORIGINAL

MOHAMMEDEEN

JEW

PERUVIAN

ALEUTIAN

GUANCHE

TASMANIAN

CIRCASSIAN

BERBER

DANDY

AFGHAN

NEW GUINEA-MAN

TEUTON

CAUCASIAN

FEJEE-
ISLANDER

MALAY

SANDWICH-
ISLANDER

JAVANESE

LAPLANDER

ESKIMAUX

CREOLE NEGRO

YOUNG
CHIMPANZEE

PHOENICIAN

MONGOL

HOTTENTOT

TARTAR

SCHILLER

A GLOSSARY OF RACIAL EPITHETS
WITH SUGGESTIONS FOR
ADDITIONAL SLURS

3/5er — *A black person. Referring to the relative value of a black person, compared to a white person.*

8 Ball — *A black person. An eight ball in billiards is black in color, as is a black person.*

8 Rock — *A very black person. A black rock is, by definition, even blacker than a black billiards ball.*

— *A* —

Abdelnaby — *An Arab person. After Alaa Abdelnaby, the Duke University basketball forward. Many racial slurs are based on the Duke basketball program.*

Abie — *A Jewish person. Derived from the name "Abraham," after the American president who freed the Jews from slavery.*

Abbo — *An aboriginal Australian. Because "aboriginal" is too much of a mouthful.*

Adolf — *A German person. After hanged war criminal Adolf Eichmann, because of Germans' passion for autoerotic asphyxiation.*

Ahab — *An Arab person. From the Ray Stevens song "Ahab the Arab." Arabs are also sometimes referred to as "Streaks."*

Alabama Blue Gums — *A black person. Bright, turquoise-colored gums are a recessive trait in many southern blacks.*

Alabama Porch Monkey — *A black person. Black people are frequently compared to simians, and front porches are an important luxury to southern black home buyers.*

Albino — *A white person, or a light-skinned black person. A bastardization of "Aldo," after Aldo Kelrast, the former stalker of comic strip doyenne Mary Worth.*

Alien Race — *Any non-Aryan person. Because Aryans are the only true natives of the planet Earth.*

Alligator Bait (or Gator Bait) — *A black person. Especially one in a swampy clime, where they are liable to be eaten by an alligator. (Also applies to members of any other race who find themselves in such a situation.)*

Amo — *An Amish person. While it is an attempt to abbreviate the word "Amish," it fails to reduce the number of syllables that the speaker must pronounce.*

Angie — *An English-speaking white person, in Quebec. Stems from the Caucasian love of the '70s-era Rolling Stones.*

Anglo — *A white person. Short for "Anglican."*

Ann (or Miss Ann) — *A white woman. After Ann-Margret. White women are also sometimes referred to as "Sex Kittens."*

Ape — *A black person. Black people, like apes, know sign language.*

Apple — *An Injun who has lost touch with his heritage. ("Red on the outside, white on the inside.") This epithet is offensive, because it assumes a red apple, despite the fact that the most delicious apples are green or yellow in color.*

Apu — *A person of subcontinental descent. (See also, "Azaria.")*

A-rab — *An Arab person. It is not clear why this is a slur.*

Arkie — *A white person of rural extraction. Because Noah and his wife were both white. The other races all evolved from the animals they took with them.*

Armo — *A white person of Armenian descent. Come on, "Armenian"? Try saying that three times fast!*

Asfalt — *A black person, in Poland. Meaning, literally, "asphalt." Because there are no black people in Poland, the Poles' only frame of reference for "things that are black" are things like asphalt and coffee grounds.*

Asshole — *An Indian person. Because Indian people are assholes.*

Aunt Jemima — *A black woman who panders to whites. So called for her sweet, syrupy demeanor around white people.*

Aunt Tomasina — *An Asian woman who kisses up to whites. A sellout. ("Aunt Tomasina" is the most popular brand of maple syrup in the Philippines.)*

Aussie Wuzzie — *A black, in Australia. Because they are adorable.*

— *B* —

Babalu — *A Hispanic person. After the signature song of Desi Arnaz, cofounder of Desilu studios.*

Baboushka — *An Eastern European or Russian woman. This slur is actually onomatopoeic.*

Babu — *An Indian. An abbreviation of "Babar," the most famous of all Indians.*

Baby Herman — *A Toon.*

Bagel Dog — *A Jewish person. After the Jewish delicacy, in which a frankfurter is stuck through the hole in a bagel.*

Baguette — *A French person. Many slurs are based on a race's traditional diet, like calling an Asian person "Rice" or a gay person "Cobb Salad."*

Balki — *A Slavic person, like television's Bronson Pinchot. Also sometimes known as "Serges."*

Bamboo Coon — *An Asian person. Because Asians are associated with the red panda, a small mammal that looks like a cross between a raccoon and a panda.*

BAP — *A black woman ("black African princess"). Because of black women's fondness for vinyl pants and Martin Landau.*

Barbie — *A blonde, white woman. Particularly one that is eight feet tall with pointy, size EE breasts.*

Bar Code — *A Jewish person. Because Jewish people like material things so much that they actually get product UPC symbols tattooed on their inner arms.*

BBK ("Big Black Kock") — *A black man's penis, from the Korn song "B.B.K." Korn has done so much to further the dialogue on this subject.*

Beaner — *A Hispanic person. Because of their aggressive pitching style.*

Benny — *A Jewish person. Many slurs are based on common first names, like "Benjamin" among Jews, "Paco" among Hispanics, or "Professor" among whites.*

Beulah — *A black woman who panders to whites. The sort of black person who would appear on a show called* Fibber McGee and Molly.

Bindi — *An Indian person. Because of India's geographical proximity to Australia, the home of Crocodile Hunter daughter Bindi Irwin.*

Big Momma — *An overweight black woman. After the Martin Lawrence film. Blacks are also sometimes known as "Black Knights" or "Wild Hogs."*

Big Nose — *A Jewish person. Because Jewish people have big noses. This epithet has also been applied to Injuns, Romans, and elephants.*

Bigger Thomas — *A black person. Because, due to societal factors, black people are not responsible for the crimes they commit.*

Bin Laden — *An Arab person. Because Arabs are very tall.*

Bird Shit (or Bird Turd) — *A white person. Because bird excrement is white. Also, if either a white person or a bird shit lands on you, it is an unpleasant experience, but one that is supposed to bring good luck.*

Black _____ — *A black person. You can add anything after "black" and make it about black people (e.g., Black Dracula, Black Frankenstein, Black Godfather of Disco, Black Jeremy Irons).*

Black Beauty — *A black person. Coined by Archie Bunker, to describe his favorite stimulant.*

Black Irish — *An Irish person with dark features, or a black person from Ireland.*

Blackanese — *A half-black, half-Asian person, like* Black Samurai *star Jim Kelly.*

Blackamoor — *A black person. Combining "black" and "moor," with an "a" in the middle to create an entirely new word.*

Blade — *A black person. Especially one who is half vampire.*

Blanket Ass — *An Injun. Smallpox can have a devastating effect on the buttocks.*

Bloodsucker — *A Jewish person, or a vampire, or a Jewish vampire.*

BLT — *A black person. Stands for "Big Lips Tyrone" or "Black Like Tar" or "Bacon, Lettuce, and Tomato."*

Blue-Eyed Devil — *A white person. Because most white people attend Duke University.*

Bog Trotter — *An Irish person. After the unsuccessful Irish trickbasketball team.*

Bohunk — *A person from Eastern Europe. A contraction of "Bohemian" and "Hungarian." Take that, Eastern Europeans.*

Boofer — *A black person, in Hawaii. A "boof" is a silent fart.*

Boogaboo — *A black person. Short for "boogety-boogety-boo," because black people are scary.*

Border Jumper — *A Hispanic person. Because of their athletic attempts at immigration.*

Boris — *A Russian person. After Pushkin's classic play, Boris Godunov, which no one has ever actually read, but is quite famous nonetheless.*

Bootlip — *A black person. Blacks have thick, leathery lips that sometimes house promiscuous old women and their countless children.*

Boy — *A black man. Or a young man of any race, really.*

Brother — *A black person. Because of all the inbreeding.*

Brougham — *A white person from the Victorian era. An archaic form of "bro-ham" or "bro-heim."*

Brown Sugar — *A black woman. Because black women are known for sleeping with Mick Jagger.*

Brownie — *A black person. Because countless black girls, aged seven to eleven, have learned how to bake cookies and jump rope thanks to the generosity and vision of Lord Baden-Powell.*

Bubba — *A white person of rural extraction. Derived from the name of the most popular white musician, Bubba Sparxxx.*

Buck — *A black person. As in, "big, black buck." Blacks are notoriously fond of both the writing and the comic acting of Buck Henry.*

Buckwheat — *A young black boy. After that beloved Little Rascal, Alfalfa.*

Buddenbrook — *A German person. The Germans are extremely difficult to read.*

Buffalo Beaner — *An Injun. Just as Hispanics eat beans, Injuns eat buffalo wings. And beans.*

Buffalo Soldier — *A black person in uniform. Black people also enjoy eating buffalo wings*

Bug Eye — *A white person. Compared to Asians, whites' eyes are very large. Also, they are composed of thousands of individual* ommatidia — *tiny, independent photoreception units.*

Bukkake — *A Japanese person. Because "bukkake" is a Japanese word.*

Bumpkin — *A white person of rural extraction. Because of their unusual phrenology.*

Burgertime — *A Hispanic person. Because of the byzantine way in which they make hamburgers, by walking over each of the ingredients one at a time with the aid of ladders.*

Burr Head — *A black person. Many blacks are aficionados of all things related to our third vice president. Similarly, whites are sometimes known as "Calhoun Heads."*

Bushie — *A black person. This slur is a description of black peoples' hair, as well as their preferred habitat.*

Bushwhacker — *A Hispanic person. Hispanics are notoriously violent toward women.*

Butter Stinker — *A white person, in Japan. Because whites smell like butter. Also, bergamot.*

— *C* —

Cake Eater — *A white person. But really, who doesn't like cake?*

Camel Jockey — *An Arab person. Sometimes "Camel Humper" or "Camel Fucker," for the several different things that Arabs do to camels.*

Camper — *A Jewish person. Jewish summer camps are popular all over the Northeast, as well as throughout Germany and Poland.*

Cannoli Fucker — *A black person. Both for their well-documented hatred of Italians (especially actor Danny Aiello) and their perverse attraction to ricotta cheese.*

Canuck — *A Canadian person. After the Vancouver hockey team (Northwest Division champions, 2003–2004).*

Caphead — *A Jewish person. Jews wear little beanies called "yarmulkes" in order to cover their bald spots.*

Captain Stabbin — *A white person. Whites are known for their anal adventures.*

Carpetbagger — *A white person, especially one from the North. After the bags that white people use when they travel to the South, in order to better exploit the war-ravaged economy.*

Carpet Pilot — *An Arab person. Arabs are known for their ornate rugs and for their preternatural ability to fly commercial jets.*

Carlton — *A black person who acts like a white person. From "Carlton Banks," the black son of a wealthy, Los Angeles judge. (Sometimes "Alfonse.")*

Casper — *A white person. From "Casper," the cartoon character, because white people are friendly.*

Cave Bitch — *A white woman. Cavewomen were, historically, both white and ill-tempered.*

Charcoal Briquette — *A black person. Black people, like charcoal briquettes, are black and flammable.*

Charlie — *An Asian person, especially a Vietnamese one who is hiding somewhere just out of sight with an automatic rifle.*

Chav — *A white person with ostentatious taste, in Britain. Also known as a "Beckham."*

Chicano — *A Hispanic person, particularly one who was born in America and wears a wifebeater everywhere he goes.*

Chicken Fucker — *A Spanish person. A more racially sensitive slur would be* "Pollo Cabron."

Chief — *An Injun. Often only the beginning of a slur, such as "Chief Big-Nose," or "Chief Stolen-Land."*

Chigger — *A half-black, half-Asian person. Because both races are genetically linked to the harvest mite.*

Ching Chong — *An Asian person. Because of the funny way they talk. Rosie O'Donnell was spot on with this one.*

Chink — *An Asian person. Asian people are physically invulnerable, except for their small, slit-like eyes—the one "chink" in their armor.*

Chocolate Man — *A black man. "Chocolate Man" is a slur, but Chocolate Thunder was a dunking machine.*

Cholo — *A Hispanic person, and a delicious snack.*

Chowder — *A white person. Presumably referring to New England clam chowder, rather than Manhattan clam chowder, in which case it would probably be a slur against Injuns.*

Christ Killer — *A Jewish person. A group of Jews, from which all other Jews are descended, stabbed Jesus Christ to death.*

Coal Black — *A black person. Coal, like charcoal, chocolate, asphalt, brownies, and 8 balls, is black.*

Cochise — *An Injun. After the famous Apache chief, and to a lesser extent Taza, son of Cochise (played by Rock Hudson).*

Colored — *A black person. Pink, yellow, and red are not technically colors.*

Coolie — *A non-white manual laborer, usually from the subcontinent or the Caribbean. Generally refers to Indians. Not to be confused with "Coolio," which refers to a single black man.*

Coon — *A black person. Because of their bushy, striped tails (the same reason blacks are often referred to as "ring-tailed lemurs").*

Corn-Fed — *A white person of rural extraction, usually a woman. Aaron Eckhart's character, Chad, describes a naive young deaf woman in Neil LaBute's* In the Company of Men *as, "Some corn-fed bitch who'd mess her pants if you sharpened a pencil for her," because white women are prone to poor bowel control.*

Cossack — *A Russian person. Because Russians enjoy riding horses and raping Jews.*

Cotton Picker — *A black person. When shopping for clothing, blacks always go straight for the 100 percent cotton items.*

Cousin Oliver — *A Hispanic person. Because they are latecomers to the United States, and now that they are here it is a good indication that the United States has jumped the shark.*

Cracker — *A white person. Whites love the smooth, buttery taste of Ritz™.*

Crackerjack — *A British person.*

Cucaracha — *A Hispanic person. Cockroaches are a delicacy in Hispanic countries.*

Cuff — *A black person. Because of the style in which blacks wear*

their slacks. They are also sometimes referred to as "Pleats" for the same reason.

Cunt Eye — *An Asian person. Because their eyes look like sideways vaginas. The pupil is the clitoris.*

Curry — *An Indian person. Curry is a popular Indian dish. They are also sometimes referred to as "Naans," "Vindaloos," "Lassis," and "Aloo Gobis."*

— D —

Dago — *An Italian person. Short for "day-glo," in reference to their poor fashion sense.*

Darkie — *A black person. Compared to other races, blacks are darker in color.*

Dark Meat — *A black person. Blacks enjoy the moister, darker-colored meat from cooked fowl, perhaps in part because it resembles their skin tone.*

Diaperhead — *An Arab person, or an Indian person. Because their turbans are made out of cloth, like cloth diapers.*

Dinge — *A black person. Used in* To Kill a Mockingbird, *referring to the fact that blacks are inefficient house-cleaners.*

Dink — *An Asian person. In reference to the quality of the knick-knacks that Asian people sell.*

Dog Eater — *An Asian person. This epithet could just as easily be applied to Armenians or Quebecois.*

Dolemite — *A black person. After the most representative character in black culture, Rudy Ray Moore.*

Doo-Doo Brown — *A black person.*

Dot (or Dot Head) — *An Indian person. Indians are infamous for their adult acne.*

Dune Coon — *An Arab person. Arabs tend to live in arid, desert climates, and their resemblance to raccoons is a matter of biological record.*

— *E* —

Eggplant — *A black person. In the UK, black people are called "aubergines."*

Eli — *A white person. Also sometimes known as a "Princetonian."*

Eraserhead — *A black person. Because of their creepy, noirish juvenilia.*

Ese — *A Hispanic person. The same epithet is used for Romans, but spelled with an extra "s."*

— *F* —

Faggotron — *A gay robot. (See also, "Fleshbot.")*

Fan Kuei — *A white person. Chinese for "ocean ghost," a kind of ghost that is very wealthy and successful.*

Father Brown — *A black person. Specifically, a black person who is also a Jesuit detective.*

Feather (or Feather Head) — *An Injun, as opposed to an Indian ("Dot"). Referring to the Injun fondness for outdated hairstyles, like that worn by Farrah Fawcett in the 1970s.*

Fez — *An Arab person, or a crypto-foreign exchange student played by a Hispanic actor. Because Arabs are known for deflowering young actresses.*

Fig Eater — *An Arab person. Because of their aggressive insistence that Newtons™ are not cookies, but, rather, "fruit and cake."*

Filthy, Stinking Jew — *A Jewish person.*

Finger Banger — *An Armenian person. Because of their insatiable thirst for manual stimulation.*

Fish Belly — *A white person. Because of their soft, scaly stomachs.*

Flip — *An Asian person. After the famous Asian comedian, Flip Wilson.*

Floor Burger — *A Swedish person. Claes Oldenburg is the world's most famous Swede.*

FOB — *Any very recent immigrant ("fresh off the boat"). Immigrants should be refrigerated within twenty-four hours to prevent spoiling.*

Frazetta — *A muscled, rugged white person wearing a loin cloth.*

Fritz — *A German person. Because many Germans are horny, jive-talking cats. (Sometimes also referred to as "Mr. Naturals" or "Schumans the Human.")*

Frog — *A French person. Because the French eat frog legs. They actually enjoy eating the legs off of any animal, including but not limited to camels, houseflies, emus, and Muppets.*

Fur Face — *A werewolf.*

— *G* —

Gabba Gabba — *A Ramonish person. (See also, "Pinhead.")*

Gable — *A black person. Because of their roguish good looks, pencil-thin mustaches, and youthful homosexual encounters.*

Gai-Jin — *A white person, in Asia. Some foreigners use nonsense words as slurs.*

Gepp — *An Italian person (after "Geppetto"). Italian men are creepy, puppet-making pedophiles.*

Ghost — *A white person. This is based on a misconception of ghosts as white in color, when in fact they are invisible, or, in some cases, translucent.*

Goldberg — *A Jewish person. Because, in the secret Jewish head-quarters beneath the ice of Antarctica, where they run all the banks and media, the Jews have amassed their fortune in the form of giant gold-bergs.*

Golliwogg — *A black person. A bastardization of "polliwog," because blacks do not develop arms or legs until after their first year of life.*

Gomer — *A white person. Not so much a slur as a favorable comparison to the greatest of all white actors, Jim Nabors.*

Gook — *An Asian person. Asians tend to be viscous and sticky, like goo. This slur also adds a comedy "k" on the end.*

Goomba — *An Italian person. Italians are small, brown, mushroom-shaped creatures that wander around aimlessly, and shrink you if you touch them.*

Goonie — *A white person. After six white kids in Oregon who went searching for buried treasure and the white criminals who chased them. (See also, "Truffle Shuffle.")*

Goy — *A non-Jew. In Hebrew, means "clean, friendly person."*

Grape Stomper — *A French person. Because the French, like house-flies, taste with their feet.*

Greaseball — *A white person, especially one from the Mediterranean region. Other races known for being greasy: Hispanics, Arabs, Indians, Blacks, Jews, Asians, and Gypsies.*

Greedo — *A Jewish person. Because they are greedy, and because they often work as interstellar bounty hunters.*

Gringo — *A white person. Abbreviated from the phrase "green means go," because of whites' close adherence to the laws of traffic.*

Guido — *An Italian person. After "Guido," the musclebound super-hero who briefly appeared in the comic* X-Factor.

Guinea — *A black person. Equatorial Guinea is known as the cradle of black civilization.*

Guinea Hen — *A black woman. A hen is a female chicken in the same way that a woman is a female human.*

Gyp — *A Gypsy. Also used as a verb, meaning "to cheat," or "to drive down property values."*

— *H* —

Habibi — *An Arab person. Because Arabs are all about love and friendship.*

Hadji — *An Indian person. After the sidekick of Jonny Quest, and the victim of known pedophile Race Bannon.*

Hajji — *An Arab person. Many Arabs take a spiritual pilgrimage, or "hajj," to Mecca, which clearly opens them up to ridicule.*

Half-Dick — *A Jewish person. Jews have half of their penises removed at birth in a procedure known as circumcision.*

Hans — *A German person. From the character played by Alan Rickman in* Die Hard. *Also why Germans are sometimes referred to as "Severus Snapes" or "Metatrons."*

Hayseed — *A white person of rural extraction. White people love hay.*

Heeb — *A Jewish person. Short for "heebie-jeebies," because Jews are creepy.*

Hick — *A white person of rural extraction. Because of their fondness for moonshine, whites are often afflicted with the hiccups.*

High Yellow — *A light-skinned black person. Because black people are known for abusing drugs. The "yellow" part I'm not as clear on.*

Hillbilly — *A white person of rural extraction. "Billy" is a common name among whites in areas with rocky topography. In the Midwest, whites are referred to as "Plainsjeffs."*

Hitler — *A German person. Adolf Hitler was Austrian, so I'm not sure to whom this refers.*

Homey — *A black person. From "Homey the Clown," a Damon Wayans character who hit children with a sock.*

Honky — *A white person. Sometimes, racists confuse white people with geese, because both are white.*

Hooknose — *A Jewish person. Jews are also sometimes referred to as "Aquilines."*

Hoser — *A Canadian person. Canadians have been known to commit suicide by placing garden hoses in the tailpipes of their idling cars.*

House Nigger — *A black person, especially one who is "uppity." Black people who live in houses are right to be uppity, since most blacks live in condos, co-ops, or the mythical, hybrid cond-op.*

Hun — *A German person. Short for "hunk," in reference to actor Klaus Kinski.*

Husky — *An Injun from Alaska. Because they are overweight.*

Hymie — *A Jewish person. Jews are known for retaining their virginity until very late in life.*

— *I* —

Ignatz — *A Hispanic person. Because of their violent tendencies and fondness for bricks.*

Injun — *An Injun. Obviously.*

Ink Face — *A black person. Their faces are black in color, as if they had been dipped in black ink, or black paint, or any sort of black substance.*

— J —

Jack — *A white person. Because white people enjoy masturbating themselves.*

JAP — *A Jewish woman ("Jewish American Princess"). Now that Anna Nicole Smith is dead, Jews are the closest thing Americans have to royalty.*

Jap — *An Asian person. From "Japanese," but using only one-third the syllables.*

Jar-Jar — *A black person. Because George Lucas is a racist.*

Jay Walker — *A Gypsy. Because of their lack of knowledge about politics and current events, which is embarrassingly revealed when they are interviewed on late-night comedy shows.*

Jerry — *A German person. After Jerry Stiller, the popular German television personality.*

Jigaboo — *A black person. Because they like to dance, and are scary.*

Jim — *A black person. After the character from* Huckleberry Finn. *There is nothing black people enjoy more than the incisive social satire of America's greatest humorist.*

Juicy Juice — *A Jewish person. Homonym.*

Jungle Bunny — *A black person. Blacks eat and shit small, hard pellets.*

— K —

Kaffir — *A black person, in South Africa. A variation of "Kiefer," based on the common misperception that the star of 24 is black.*

Kike — *A Jewish person. Originally from the 1996 Michael Jackson song, "They Don't Care About Us," in which the Caucasian musician sang, "kick me, kike me, don't you black or white me."*

Kingfish — *An older black person. Because of their lust for power and near-dictatorial control over Louisiana politics.*

Kiwi — *A New Zealander. New Zealanders, like Kiwis, are tiny and adorable.*

Knuckle Dragger — *A black person, or caveman. Both are known for their poor posture.*

Kraut — *A German person. Germans like cabbage almost as much as they hate anthropomorphic mice, or "mäuse."*

Krzyzewski — *A Polish person. After Mike Krzyzewski, the coach of the Duke University basketball team.*

Kunta Kinte — *A black person. After the charming, non-threatening host of television's* Reading Rainbow.

$$- L -$$

Labradoodle — *A person of mixed Labrador and Poodlish descent.*

Latrino — *A Hispanic person. A combination of the words "Latino" and "latrine" to create a new word altogether. This slur implies that Hispanics go to the bathroom.*

Latke — *An Eastern European person. Eastern Europeans are 70 percent potato.*

Lawn Jockey — *A black person. Because they enjoy standing perfectly still on your front lawn, pretending to ride a horse.*

Leech — *A Jewish person. Because of the blood-drinking.*

Lefty — *An Arab person. Sometimes also called "southpaws."*

Lemonhead — *An Asian person. Because of their sour demeanors.*

Leopold and Loeber — *A Jewish person. Because Jews are child-murderers.*

Leprechaun — *An Irish person. Because of the longstanding Irish devotion to the gold standard. William Jennings Bryan is a national pariah in Ireland.*

Leroy — *A black person. After the Jim Croce song, "Bad, Bad Leroy*

Brown," in which the black protagonist is the baddest man in the whole damn town.

Limey — *A British person. English people love limes. And gin. And tonic. And ice cubes.*

Lo Faan — *A white person. Literally, "barbarian," after one of the most famous whites, Conan. Whites are also sometimes referred to as "Destroyers," or "Krulls."*

Lobsterback — *A British person. Because of the British habit of sodomizing lobsters.*

— M —

Macaca — *An Indian person. After the word that torpedoed George Allen's 2000 reelection campaign.*

Macaroni — *An Italian person. Because Italian cooking uses lots of noodles, one of which is the macaroni noodle. Also sometimes called "Spaghettis," "Fusillis," and "Farfalles."*

Mack — *A Scottish person. Because of the Scottish proclivity for pimping.*

Malakas — *A Greek person. Because it is a funny-sounding word.*

Mamasan — *An Asian woman. From "mamu," the Asian word for woman, and "san," the Asian word for woman.*

Mammy — *A large black woman. Black women have a very difficult time losing the extra weight after childbirth.*

The Man — *A white person. An honorific, as in "You da man!"*

Mandingo — *A black person. According to recent genetic research, blacks count both humans and marsupials among their ancestors.*

Mario — *An Italian person. Sometimes also called "Luigis," "Warios," and "Princess Toadstools."*

Massa — *A white person. Short for "massa of ceremonies," because of the prevalence of Caucasian rap stars.*

Mau-Mau — *A black person. From the lyrics to the black spiritual, "Surfin' Bird."*

Meatball — *An Italian person. Because of the common Italian experience of attending a raunchy summer camp.*

Meathead — *An Italian person, or a young Rob Reiner.*

Merkin — *A white person. It is nothing to be ashamed of.*

Mexican't — *A Hispanic person. Racist wordplay is some of the funniest wordplay.*

Mick — *An Irish person. Short for "Mickey," as in, "I slipped her a mickey." The Irish are notorious date rapists.*

Mo — *An Arab person. Because Arab men like to have sex with each other.*

Mocky — *A Jewish person. Jews are real wiseacres, always making fun.*

Mohammedan — *An Arab person. Because Arabs follow the teachings of the prophet, Nostradamus.*

Moishe — *A Jewish person. Some Jews have the unusual first name, "Moishe," therefore all Jews might have it.*

Moke — *A black person. A bastardization of "Mookie," from Mookie Wilson, the outfielder for the 1986 New York Mets.*

Money Lender — *A Jewish person. Based on a misunderstanding; Jews hoard money, they don't lend it out.*

Mongol — *An Asian person. Mongolia is a country in Asia.*

Monkey — *A black person. Blacks are simian-like in appearance, and known for throwing their own poop.*

Mookie — *A black person. From Mookie Blaylock, the Atlanta Hawks point guard. (Who was, in turn, named after the early Eddie Vedder band, "Mookie Blaylock.")*

Moolie — *A black person. From the Italian word for "eggplant," because blacks soak up so much oil.*

Moon Cricket — *A black person. Because sometimes, racism doesn't make any fucking sense at all.*

Moor — *A black person. Because black people are cast as Othello more than any other Shakespeare character.*

Motisa — *A black person. A joke at the expense of black servants, who are trained to ask—"mo' tea suh?" White people can't get enough tea.*

Muck — *An Injun, in Alaska. Everyone knows that Eskimos live in the snow, but people forget that snow sometimes melts. And then what are you left with?*

Mud Person — *A black person. The first blacks were made out of mud from the banks of the Moldau River.*

Mudslime — *An Arab person. Derived from "muslin," the fabric of choice for Arabs. It is common for an epithet to turn a mundane detail about a race into a slur.*

Muja — *An Arab person. From "mujahideen," the Arab word for "mujahedeen."*

Mule — *A mulatto. When a male donkey impregnates a female horse, the offspring is sterile, like a mulatto.*

Mung — *An Asian person. Because of the Asian tradition of digging up corpses and ingesting the fluids that are expelled from their genitals when pressure is applied to the belly.*

Mustard Seed — *A light-skinned black person. Because blacks are akin to the kingdom to the heaven.*

Muybridge — *An Asian person. Because of their jerky, disjointed way of walking, running, and jumping hurdles.*

Muzzie — *An Arab person. An abbreviation of "muzzle." Because of the Arab tendency to bite strangers, they are required to wear a muzzle in public.*

— N —

Nacho — *A Hispanic person. The Jack Black movie* Nacho Libre *was set in Mexico.*

Naga — *A black person ("North American Ground Ape"). Blacks may be ape-like, but they are not very good at climbing trees.*

Nappy Head — *A black person. A black person's hair, which grows out of his head, is nappy.*

Narrowback — *An Irish person. The Irish have bizarrely proportioned bodies.*

Native — *A black person. From "nativity," because in nativity scenes, Jesus is invariably black.*

Nazi — *A German person. "Nazi" is short for "national socialist," and Germans are notorious economic protectionists.*

Negress — *A black woman. Just like a female waiter is a "waitress" or a female actor is an "actress." The suffix "-ess" means, literally, "less than."*

Negro — *A black person. The anthropological term is "Negroid."*

Newfie — *A Newfoundlander. Newfoundlanders are filthy, inbred, thieving, pedophile radish farmers. They deserve worse than "Newfie."*

Nickel Nose — *A Jewish person. Just as pigs can smell out truffles, Jews use their noses to find hidden or buried coinage.*

Nig — *A black person. A combination of "negro" and "pig," because blacks are considered unclean by Jews. (They have cloven hooves, but do not chew their own cud.)*

The N-Word — *A black person.*

Niglet — *A black child. Literally, "a small nig."*

Ninny — *A black person. Because they are cowardly and effeminate.*

Nip — *An Asian person. Because of their love of the rich, creamy*

hard candy. Nestlé® NIPS® come in seven luscious flavors—Butter Rum, Caramel, Chocolate Parfait, Coffee, Dulce de Leche, Mocha, and Peanut Butter Parfait.

Norbit — *A black person. This is the most offensive anti-black slur I can think of.*

Nuprin — *An Asian person. Because Asians, like the pain-relief pills, are little, yellow, different, and nonsteroidal.*

— O —

Octaroon — *A black person. Specifically, a black person with only one black great-grandparent, but that is all it takes. A single drop of black blood dilutes the purity of an entire family tree.*

Okie — *A white person. Oklahoma is the cradle of white civilization.*

Opie — *A white person. Despite their successes later in life, whites will always be remembered for their work as child actors.*

Orange Picker — *A Hispanic person. Hispanics are some of the most ardent fans of Syracuse University's basketball program, and it is reflected in their office pool tournament brackets.*

Orangutan — *A black person. Blacks, like orangutans, are responsible for numerous murders on the Rue Morgue in Paris.*

Oreo — *A black person who has lost touch with his heritage. An Oreo is "black on the outside, white on the inside," much like Oreo spokesperson Randy Jackson.*

Oriental — *An Asian person. Because Asians are from the mysterious lands of the darkest Orient.*

Osama — *An Arab person. "Osama" is a common Arab name, like "Moqtada" or "Saddam."*

Oyster Cracker — *A Merperson. Because they look like whites from the waist up, but live underwater.*

— P —

Packer — *A white person. After Billy Packer, the most revered of all white people.*

Paddy — *An Irish person. Because of the Irish reliance on the rice crop.*

Pakeha — *A white person. (Maori for "white devil.") Self-explanatory.*

Paki — *An Indian person. From "Pac-Man," because of Indians' insatiable appetite for glowing dots.*

Paisan — *An Italian person. "Paisan" is the sound of a bullet being shot through a silencer.*

Paleface — *A white person. Compared to the other races, whites appear pale, especially in the facial region.*

Pancake Face — *An Asian person. Because Asians have round, flat faces. And you know what else is round and flat? Pancakes. Q.E.D.*

Panda — *A mulatto. Specifically, one who is white, but with big splotches of black on the arms, legs, ears, and over the eyes.*

Papasan — *An Asian man. Asian men are infamous for sitting in rounded, bowl-shaped chairs.*

Pasty Face — *A white person. In the vaudeville era, minstrel performers would use a thick, white paste in order to appear Caucasian for their whiteface acts.*

Patel — *An Indian person. Actually an acronym, for "Preternaturally Adept Trapezists, Etymologists, and Lepidopterists." Apparently, Indians are exceptionally talented in these three pursuits.*

Patinkin — *A white person. After Mandy.*

Peckerwood — *A white person. From the uniquely Caucasian sexual fetish of fucking trees.*

Pedro — *A Hispanic person. Because of their fondness for the young actor, Efren Ramirez, especially his breakout role in 2004's* Napoleon Dynamite.

Pepé Le Pew — *A French person. The French are cat-rapers.*

Pepperbelly — *A Hispanic person. Because of the Hispanic love for spicy foods. They are also sometimes referred to as "Ulcers," "Heartburns," and "Burning Rectums."*

Peppermint Patty — *An Irish woman. Because of their tendency towards Lesbianism.*

Perker — *An Arab person. A bastardization of "porker," because of the chronic obesity that is endemic among many Arab populations.*

Pickaninny — *A black person. Because blacks are famous for being incompetent team captains in gym class. They invariably choose the least qualified teammates.*

Pig — *A white person. The vestigial tails that all humans have (the "tailbone") is more pronounced in whites, and sometimes forms a subtle corkscrew shape. Also, most police officers are white.*

Piker — *A Gypsy. Gypsies in Britain often use long, pointed sticks to remove their victims' wallets.*

Pilgrim — *A white person. All whites are descended from the original pilgrims, who sailed to America on the* Mayflower. *Caucasians are also referred to as "Massachusettsians," or "Massholes."*

Pie Face — *An Asian person. Pies, like pancakes, are round and relatively flat.*

Pineapple — *An Asian person, especially a Pacific Islander. Not because of the prevalence of pineapples in that region, but because of the scaly, yellow skin of its inhabitants.*

Pinewood — *A white person. Because whites dominate the Cub Scouts, and therefore the Pinewood Derby.*

Ping-Pong — *An Asian person. Asians both talk funny and are champion table tennis players.*

Pinko — *A Russian person. The harsh winters of Russia can be very hard on one's skin.*

Pinto — *A Hispanic person. Many Hispanics were duped into buying Ford Pintos in the 1970s, based on their fondness for the bean of the same name.*

Pogue — *An Irish person. Specifically, Shane MacGowan.*

Polack (or "Polock") — *A Polish person. After the ancestral forebear of the Polish people: Count Polock, a mentally retarded vampire.*

Pom — *A British person. Frequently used in South Africa and Australia, "pom" is short for "pomegranate," which is rhyming slang for "immigrant." Sometimes also called "Maggots" or "Clock Shuckers."*

Ponch — *A Hispanic person. Because of the beer belly that Hispanic men develop after years of riding with the California Highway Patrol.*

Poodle — *A white person. Whites are known for their lustrous coats and their prissy manner.*

Potato Eater — *An Irish person. Because of their fondness for the early work of Vincent van Gogh.*

Powder — *A white person. Because of the white obsession with putting Gold Bond® on their balls.*

Pubie — *A black person. For some unknown reason, blacks grow an extraordinary amount of pubic hair. (This is also why black men are sometimes called "Bushmen.")*

Punjab — *An Indian person. When Indian women greet each other, they do so by punching the other woman in the vagina.*

— Q —

Quahog — *A white woman from New England. Because they are larger than the women found in other regions.*

Quadroon — *A black person with only one black grandparent. Still too black to be president.*

Quintroon — *A black person with only one black great-great-grandparent. Still too black to be president.*

— R —

Rabbit — *A black person. Because of the quick, pleasureless manner in which they perform intercourse.*

Raghead — *An Arab person. Or an Indian person. Or a homeless person.*

Raisinette — *A black child. You never really think about black children except when you go to the movies.*

Raisin Head — *A black person. Underneath their nappy hair, black peoples' scalps are wrinkled and puckered like a raisin.*

Redbone — *A light-skinned black person. From Leon Redbone, the man who wrote and performed the* Mr. Belvedere *theme song. Black people often drop kick their jackets when they walk in a door.*

Redman — *An Injun. After the rapper. Injuns smoke a lot of marijuana.*

Redneck — *A white person. The etymology of this slur is unclear, as it should really refer to an Injun instead.*

Redskin — *An Injun. For you see, Injuns have red skin.*

Reggin — *A black person. (Spells "the N-Word" backward.) This elaborate code was only broken in 1822, by Frenchman Jean-François Champollion.*

Rex Morgan, M.D. — *A white person. Because white people are incredibly boring.*

Ricky Ricardo — *A Hispanic person. After the Hispanic minstrel character played by Desi Arnaz on* I Love Lucy.

Rice Eater — *An Asian person. Rice is a dietary staple in most Asian countries. Not to be confused with the Hispanic slur, "Red Beans and Rice Eater."*

Rico (or "Rico Suave") — *A Hispanic person. Gerardo has long been the unofficial spokesman of the Hispanic community.*

Round Eye — *A white person. Just as dogs are colorblind, and Jews see only infrared, whites view the world as if they were looking through a fish-eye lens.*

Round Hair — *A black person. Look at a black person's hair under a microscope, and you'll see that it's made up of thousands of tiny, perfectly round crystals.*

Rug Rider — *An Arab person. Arab society can be sexually repressive, and some Arab men must resort to engaging in intercourse with whatever household items happen to be around.*

Russkie — *A Russian person. A transliteration of the Russian word "Русский," which means, literally, "Russian." It is unclear how a word spelled P-Y-C-C-K-Backwards-N-Backwards-N-with-an-umlaut-over-it is pronounced "Russkie," but the Russians are a mysterious people.*

— S —

Saltine — *A white person. A crude slur based on the white love of* fleur de sel.

Sambo — *A black person. After Rufus Sambo, the gently retarded Southern black man. (Also sometimes referred to as "Wesley Willises.")*

Sand Nigger — *An Arab person. Imagine someone lives in the desert.* Now imagine he's black.

Sapphire — *A black woman. Because black women are shiny and of particular significance to people born in September.*

Scarecrow — *A black person. Birds are scared of black people. As are white people, dogs, and babies.*

Schlitzauge — *An Asian person, in Germany (literally, "slit-eyed"). The Germans are capable of turning the most complex concept into a single word.*

Schvartzer — *A black person. Specifically, a black Jew. (See "Whoopi Goldberg.")*

Scooby — *A black person. Because of their love of scat.*

Scratchback — *A Hispanic person. Many Hispanics have been bankrupted by the easy promises and false hope of instant lottery games.*

Seat Filler — *A Hispanic person. Because that is the only way that Hispanic people are allowed to attend fancy awards shows.*

Shadow Cat — *A black person. Black people, like shadows, are dark in color, and, like Kitty Pride, they can walk through walls.*

Shaniqua — *A black woman. Specifically, one named Shaniqua.*

Sharp — *A white person. Because white people are on the ball. They're crackerjack.*

Sheenie — *A Jewish person. Because it is a silly, vaguely Hebraic-sounding word. Like "Schphitz" or "Schtikl" or "Adonai."*

Shine — *A black person. (See "Sapphire.")*

Shylock — *A Jewish person. After the Shakespeare character, a predatory money lender, because of the premium that Jews place on a liberal arts education that includes Elizabethan drama.*

Shyster — *A Jewish person. A jocular modernization of "Shylock," coined by prominent racist Rob Schneider.*

Silk Spinner — *An Asian person. Asians secrete a silk-like substance that is harvested from their larvae.*

Silverback — *A large black man. Because black men, like silverback gorillas, receive a lot of attention from white women, like Dian Fossey.*

Skunk — *An Arab person. Because Arabs love beer, but there are limited options for refrigeration in the desert.*

Slit Eye (or "Slant Eye") — *An Asian person. A polite form of the more common "Shit Eye," because of Asians' poor eyesight.*

Slope — *A black person. After the Park Slope region of Brooklyn, in New York City. A popular epithet, even though no black people actually live in Park Slope.*

Snowman — *A white person. Because white people are white, like snow, and have pointy, carrot-like noses.*

Sootie — *An Indian person. When Indians emigrate to Great Britain, the only work they can find is sweeping chimneys.*

Spade — *A black person. From the phrase, "as black as the ace of spades," but also in reference to blacks' weapon of choice.*

Spearchucker — *A black person. After Captain Oliver "Spearchucker" Jones, a field surgeon during the Korean War.*

Spic — *A Hispanic person. Abbreviations like these can be a real time-saver.*

Spizzwink(?) — *A white person. And yes, the name includes the question mark.*

Spook — *A black person. Black people are a common attraction in haunted houses.*

Spoon Face — *An Asian person. From the Soundgarden song, "Spoonman," which was featured on the soundtrack to the movie* Singles. *The Asian love of Matt Dillon is well documented.*

Squaw — *An Injun woman. Short for "squawk," because, as any brave will tell you, Injun women do not shut up.*

Squinty — *An Asian person. Asians are known for their poor eyesight and their resistance to Western innovations in optics.*

Struwwelpeter — *A black person. Because their afro hairdos make them appear "shock-headed."*

Sushi Dick — *An Asian person. After the popular Japanese dish.*

— *T* —

Taco Bender — *A Hispanic person. Hispanics enjoy eating tacos almost as much as they like destroying them.*

Taffy — *A Welsh person. The Welsh are ridiculed around the world for their love of inferior "freshwater" taffy.*

Tape Head — *An Asian person. Asians are huge King's X fans.*

Tar Baby — *A black person. Because black babies are covered with a sticky, mucous-like lining for their first several years of life.*

Teabag — *A British person. It is an open secret that the British enjoy having testicles gently lowered onto their faces.*

Tee-Pee Creeper — *An Injun. Also the name of the only car ever produced by the Injun Motor Corporation (IMC).*

Terrorist — *An Arab person. Not so much a slur as a synonym.*

Three-Namer — *A white person. Because of the prevalence of white assassins (Lee Harvey Oswald, James Earl Ray, John Wilkes Booth, &c).*

Tommy — *A British person. After Thomas Kinkade, Painter of Light. The British have terrible taste in art.*

Tonto — *An Injun. Because all Injuns act and talk just like character actor Jay Silverheels.*

Toto — *A black person. Because they bless the rains down in Africa.*

Towel Head — *An Arab person. Arab hair takes a very long time to dry.*

Trajan — *An Injun person, in Alaska. After the Alaskan Assassin, Trajan Langdon.*

Twinkie — *An Asian person who has lost touch with his heritage. Because Asians are spongy.*

Tulip Eater — *An Arab person. Because of their contentious relationship with the Netherlands.*

Two-Fister — *A white person. Because of their hard-hitting, tough-talking war stories.*

— U —

Uncle Miltie — *A Jewish person. Because of their huge schlongs.*

Uncle Tom — *A black person who panders to white people. After the novel by Harriet Beecher Stowe, which also gave its name to the African American wing of the Republican Party: Uncle Tom's Cabin Republicans.*

— V —

Vampire — *A Jewish person. Because Jews burn very easily in the sun.*

Vanilla Face — *A white person. Vanilla beans are small, black pods that are found in certain species of orchids. I am not sure I understand this epithet.*

Velcro Head — *A black person. Based on experiments that NASA performed in the 1970s.*

Voltron — *A shape-changing giant mecha robot.*

— W —

Wagon Burner — *An Injun. Because a large segment of the Injun population carries the arson gene on their eighteenth chromosome.*

Wahoo — *An Injun. Because Injuns are easily excitable, and make excellent crowd members at sporting events.*

Wasp — *A white person. Whites, like wasps, are naturally drawn to the healing waters of Cape Cod.*

Water Buffalo — *A black person. Because, according to the University of Pennsylvania, water buffaloes are from Africa. Even though they are from Asia.*

Watermelon Eater — *A black person. Because black people enjoy the sweet, refreshing taste of watermelons. Other races who enjoy watermelon: all of them.*

Welfare Monkey — *A black person, or a simian who collects disability.*

Wetback — *A Hispanic person. Hispanics are often so desperate for a nap that they will nod off against a freshly painted wall.*

Weird Beard — *A Jewish person. "Weird Beard" was the first and only Jewish pirate.*

Whiffenpoof — *A white person. Pretty much any a cappella group's name can be a synonym for "white." Other good examples include the Krokodiloes, the Penny Loafers, the Logarhythms, and the Tigertones. (Though "Nassoon," after the Princeton Nassoons, is actually a slur against Bahamians.)*

White Bread — *A white person. If races were breads, whites would be white bread, Jews would be rye, and blacks would be pumpernickel. Asians would probably be potato bread.*

White Devil — *A white person. The white devil is a lesser, generally harmless demon, just as a white lie is less objectionable than a regular lie.*

White Meat — *A white person. Based on a misconception, since all humans are technically red meat. (I recommend a mellow merlot*

or pinot noir as an accompaniment, to offset the strong, gamy taste of the meat.)

White Trash — *A white person of rural extraction. Because whites tend to be more wasteful than the other races.*

Whitey — *A white person. After Whitey Ford, the New York Yankees pitcher. (This is a holdover from an era when baseball was associated with white people, rather than Hispanics and Asians.)*

Wife-Fucker — *A Norwegian person. Norwegian men are notoriously faithful husbands.*

Wigger — *A white person who tries to act like a black person. Because of whites' naturally smooth, luxuriant hair, these individuals must often wear wigs to simulate the coarse, nappy hair of a black person.*

Wing Ding — *A black person. For their love of both chicken and eclectic fonts. (See also, "Zapf Dingbat.")*

Wool Head — *A black person. Blacks are actually genetically closer to sheep than humans. Specifically, black sheep.*

Wop — *An Italian person. For "without papers," because Italians are notoriously bad with forms and receipts.*

— *X* —

X — *A black person. MDMA abuse has reached epidemic levels in the black community.*

— *Y* —

Yam-Yam — *A black person. From the Turkish for "cannibal," after Roland Gift, the half-black lead singer of the Fine Young Cannibals.*

Yard Ape — *A black person. The yard ape is a small, domesticated simian similar to the gibbon.*

Yellow Man — *An Asian person. Because of the Asian love of reggae.*

Yergacheffe — *A black person. Because they are exploited by the Starbucks corporation.*

Yid — *A Jewish person. From "Yid Army," the legion of fans of the London soccer team, the Tottenham Spurs.*

Yoko — *An Asian woman. After Yoko Ono, the accomplished musician and artist, who was an early member of the Fluxus movement and was tangentially connected to the British music scene in the 1960s and '70s.*

Yolk — *An Asian person. The yolk of an egg is the yellow part.*

Yo-Yo — *A black person. Because of the most popular hobby among urban blacks.*

— Z —

Zeke — *An Asian person. "Zeke" is short for "Ezekiel," which still doesn't make sense.*

Zembo — *A Zemblan person, from the distant, northern land.*

Zip Coon — *A black person. Specifically, a zany, zoot suit–wearing black, who sings happy songs all de live long day.*

Zoghal — *A black person. Literally, "coal," in Persian. After the Farsi version of the Warner Brothers cartoon,* Coal Black and de Sebben Dwarfs.

Zot — *A black person. From police officers' slang, after the sound a taser makes.*

INDEX

HANDBOOKS BY THE SAME AUTHOR

HOW TO WRITE;
A NEW POCKET MANUAL of Composition and Letter Writing, with Hints on Penmanship and Writing Materials, and Practical Rules for Literary Composition, Newspaper Writing, Punctuation and Proof Correcting, etc.
Price, paper, 80 c.; cloth, 50 cents.

HOW TO TALK;
A NEW POCKET MANUAL of Conversation and Debate, with Directions for Acquiring a Grammatical and Graceful Style; with more than Five Hundred Common Mistakes Corrected.
Price, paper, 80 c.; cloth, 50 cents.

HOW TO BEHAVE;
A NEW POCKET MANUAL of Republican Etiquette, and Guide to Correct Personal Habits; with Rules for Debating Societies and Deliberative Assemblies.
Price, paper, 80 c.; cloth, 50 cents.

HOW TO WOO;
A NEW POCKET MANUAL of Courtship and Guide to Proper Romantic Technique; with Directions for Dinner Conversation and the Physical Act of Love. With Hundreds of Illustrations for Instruction and Personal Use.
Price, paper, 80 c.; cloth, 50 cents.

HOW TO DO BUSINESS;
A NEW POCKET MANUAL of Practical Affairs and Guide to Success in Life; with a Collection of Business Forms and a Dictionary of Commercial Terms.
Price, paper, 80 c.; cloth, 50 cents.

HOW TO GOVERN;
A NEW POCKET MANUAL of Politics and Leadership at the State, Municipal, and Federal Levels; with a Selection of Sample Legislation and Common Ethical Mistakes.
Price, paper, 80 c.; cloth, 50 cents.

HOW TO SLEEP;
A NEW POCKET MANUAL of Dozing, and Guide to Proper Breathing and Posture; with Hints on Napping and Slumber. Including Exercises to Prevent Somnambulation and Night Screaming.
Price, paper, 80 c.; cloth, 50 cents.

THE GARDEN;
A NEW POCKET MANUAL of Practical Horticulture; or, How to Cultivate Vegetables, Fruits, and Flowers. With a Chapter on Ornamental Trees and Shrubs.
Price, paper, 80 c.; cloth, 50 cents.

THE FARM;
A NEW POCKET MANUAL of Practical Agriculture; or, How to Cultivate all the Field Crops. With an Essay on Farm Management, etc.
Paper, 80 c.; muslin, 50 cents.

DOMESTIC ANIMALS;
A NEW POCKET MANUAL of Cattle, Horse, and Sheep Husbandry, etc.
Price, paper, 80 c.; cloth, 50 cents.

THE IRISH;
A NEW POCKET MANUAL of Guineas, Micks, and Paddys; or, How to Feed and Care for the Irish and their Families. With several Harrowing Illustrations.
Price, paper, 80 c.; cloth, 50 cents.

In Preparation
THE HOUSE;
A NEW POCKET MANUAL of Rural Architecture.
Price, paper, 80 c.; cloth, 50 cents.

Sent to any Post-Office by Return mail, on Receipt of the Price.

"There are plenty of good reasons for fighting, but no good reason ever to hate without reservation, to imagine that God Almighty Himself hates with you, too."

Kurt Vonnegut

ACKNOWLEDGMENTS

Thanks to Daniel Immerwahr, the voice of reason, without whom this book would be 75 percent worse.

Thanks also to my family for their support, and to the staff of *The Daily Show,* for their tolerance.